Concept Modules with Note Taking and Practice Exams

FOR COON AND MITTERER'S PSYCHOLOGY: MODULES FOR ACTIVE LEARNING, ELEVENTH EDITION

CLAUDIA COCHRAN

El Paso Community College

SHAWN TALBOT

Kellogg Community College

THOMSON

WADSWORTH

Australia · Brazil · Canada · Mexico · Singapore · Spain
United Kingdom · United States

THOMSON

™

WADSWORTH

Concept Modules with Note Taking and Practice Exams for Coon and Mitterer's Psychology: Modules for Active Learning
Claudia Cochran/Shawn Talbot

Psychology Editor: Jaime Perkins
Development Editor: Jeremy Judson
Assistant Editor: Magnolia Molcan
Editorial Assistant: Wilson Co
Technology Project Manager: Bessie Weiss
Marketing Manager: Sara Swangard
Marketing Assistant: Melanie Cregger
Marketing Communications Manager: Linda Yip
Project Manager, Editorial Production: Jerilyn Emori
Creative Director: Rob Hugel

Art Director: Vernon Boes
Print Buyer: Karen Hunt
Permissions Editor: Bob Kauser
Production Service: Carol O'Connell, Graphic World Inc.
Text Designer: Diane Beasley
Photo Researcher: Kathleen Olson
Cover Designer: Larry Didona
Cover Image: ©Panoramic Images/Getty Images
Compositor: Graphic World Inc.

Printed in Canada
1 2 3 4 5 6 7 11 10 09 08 07

Thomson Higher Education
10 Davis Drive
Belmont, CA 94002-3098
USA

Student Edition:
ISBN-13: 978-0-495-50709-3
ISBN-10: 0-495-50709-1

For more information about our products, contact us at:
Thomson Learning Academic Resource Center
1-800-423-0563
For permission to use material from this text or product, submit a request online at **http://www.thomsonrights.com.**
Any additional questions about permissions can be submitted by e-mail to **thomsonrights@thomson.com.**

Contents

Preface

To the Student

This booklet is a study tool designed to help you better understand essential chapter concepts. For each chapter, this booklet provides a visual guide of each module, designated space for note taking, and a practice exam consisting of 20 multiple-choice questions.

Concept Modules with Note Taking

Research has shown that, for some learners, presenting information in a visual format improves retention of material. The concept modules began several years ago with an individual instructor's attempt to give students a study tool in an alternative format that allowed them to review information as they prepared for examinations. Many of you will find the concept modules extremely helpful from the very beginning of your course. For others, you may discover their value as you proceed with your studies.

How do you make use of these concept modules? The Introduction to the main text discusses how to study psychology and explains the SQ4R method (a quick synopsis is also provided here). These visual guides are an integral part of the "S" ("Survey") and one of the "R's" ("Review").

Survey

Even before you survey the chapter, survey the concept modules. A preview like this gives you an overview of what material will be covered and highlights some key concepts that you will want to focus on.

Review

After you have read the chapter and want to test your mastery of the material, use the concept modules for review. At each point along the way, ask yourself:

- How much do I now know about each topic discussed here?
- What information do I now know that was not included in the concept modules?
- What items would I have added if I had been the creator of the concept modules?
- What questions is my instructor likely to ask about the topics that have been presented?

Space is provided for students who find it helpful to make detailed notes as they progress through the chapters.

Finally, the practice exams, found at the end of each chapter's concept modules, serve as a good overall review of the major points in each chapter

Practice Exams

After going through the concept modules and writing notes about key concepts in the chapters, you will encounter a practice exam. The practice exams consist of 20 multiple-choice questions that test your knowledge of the chapters' main themes. Answers to the practice exams are located in the back of this booklet.

We hope that you find these *Concept Modules with Note Taking and Practice Exams* a valuable study tool in mastering your course material.

Chapter 1

MODULE 1.1

The Science of Psychology

Psychology is the scientific study of behavior and mental processes. Psychologists seek empirical evidence based on scientific observation.

Psychology
Scientific study of
- Behavior
- Mental processes

Behaviors
- Eating
- Sleeping
- Talking
- Walking

Mental Processes
- Thoughts
- Memories
- Emotions
- Dreams

Four Goals of Psychology

1. Describe
What is happening?

2. Understand
Why is it happening?

3. Predict
When will it happen?

4. Control
Can it be changed?

MODULE 1.2

Critical Thinking and the Scientific Method in Psychology

The Scientific Method

1. Observe
Computer game designers have varying levels of stress.

2. Define the Problem
In what ways are high stress and low stress game designers different?
High control vs. Low control?

3. Propose the Hypothesis
Game designers who have *more control* over difficult tasks will report *less* stress.

4. Gather the Evidence and Test the Hypothesis
Ramdomly assign subjects into two groups:
1. Forced pace (low control) = high stress
2. Self pace (high control) = low stress

5. Publish Results
Write and publish a scholarly article. Describe the research question, the methods, the results, and the conclusions.

6. Build Theories
Use the results from this and other experiments to create a theory that explains why having control over a task reduces stress.

Introducing Psychology and Research Methods

History and Contemporary Perspectives

Psychology began as a branch of philosophy, which includes the study of knowledge, reality, and human nature. Psychology developed as a science when the scientific method began to be applied.

Modern Psychological Perspectives

Biological

Based on biological principles
- Brain processes
- Evolution
- Genetics
- Neuroscience

Careers

Biopsychologists
Evolutionary psychologists

Psychological

Based on psychological principles
- Objective observation
- Mental processes
- Humanistic view
- Psychodynamic view

Careers

Cognitive psychologists
Psychodynamic psychologists

Sociocultural

Based on social and cultural principles
- Multiculturalism
- Universal behaviors
- Cultural relativity
- Social norms

Careers

Crosscultural psychologists

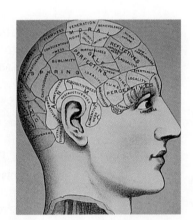

Psychologists and Their Specialties

Myths

Facts

Psychologists are all shrinks.

→ "Shrinks" are psychiatrists, not psychologists. Psychologists hold master's or doctorate degrees. Psychologists are trained in psychological
- Methods
- Knowledge
- Theories

Psychologists are more disturbed than their patients.

→ Psychologists are often inaccurately portrayed in the media.
Psychologists are responsible and hardworking.
Psychologists follow an ethical code and must respect people's privacy, dignity, confidentiality, and welfare.

Most psychologists are therapists in private practice.

→ ONLY 16 percent of psychologists work in clinical settings. Most psychologists work in varied settings:
- Teaching
- Research
- Administer psychological tests
- Serving as consultants

Psychologists, psychiatrists, social workers, counselors . . . what's the difference?

→ Clinical psychologists have a Ph.D or Psy.D. and treat mental disorders through psychotherapy.
Counseling psychologists have a master's degree and treat milder problems at school or work.
Psychiatrists are medical doctors (M.D.s), and also treat mental disorders, often through drug therapy.
Psychiatric social workers have an M.S.W and assist both psychologists and psychiatrists as part of a team.

The Psychology Experiment

The Psychology Experiment

1. Directly vary a condition, called the independent variable
2. Create two or more groups of subjects (using random assignment)
3. Record whether

   the **independent variable (IV)**

   causes an effect on

   the **dependent variable (DV)**

Group 1
Experimental Group
- Receives the IV
- All other conditions are kept the same

Group 2
Control Group
- Does not receive the IV
- All other conditions are kept the same

Compare the Results
Did the results of the experimental group differ significantly from the control?
  If yes, then the IV caused the differences (reject the null hypothesis).
  If no, then the IV had no effect (accept the null hypothesis).

Notes

_____

_____

_____

_____

_____

_____

_____

_____

Nonexperimental Research Methods

Naturalistic Observation
Observing behavior in natural settings

Clinical Method/Case Studies
Studying psychological problems in clinical settings

Surveys
Using questionnaires to poll large groups

Correlation Studies
Studying the relationships between events

Psychology in Action: Psychology in the Media
How to tell fact from fiction.

Suggestion 1
Be skeptical.

Suggestion 5
Observation or interference?

Suggestion 2
How credible is the source?

Suggestion 6
Oversimplification?

Suggestion 3
Was there a control group?

Suggestion 7
Overgeneralization?

Suggestion 4
Correlation or causation?

1. Information gained through direct observation is known as
   a. empirical evidence.
   b. overt behaviors.
   c. covert behaviors.
   d. scientific observation.

2. If you are studying issues such as how people deal with death and dying, you may be considered a(n) _____ psychologist.
   a. social
   b. forensic
   c. developmental
   d. evolutionary

3. Psychology's goals include all of the following except
   a. control.
   b. observe.
   c. describe.
   d. predict.

4. Ray observes that more batters are hit by pitched balls on hot days than on cold days. His explanation for this is that the heat makes the pitchers more aggressive. This explanation is an example of a(n)
   a. theory.
   b. fallacy.
   c. hypothesis.
   d. assumption.

5. If Ray then specifies that "hot" means above 90° F, we would say he has _____ "hot."
   a. operationally defined
   b. systematically defined
   c. inappropriately defined
   d. explicitly defined

6. _____ is often referred to as the father of psychology.
   a. Dennis Coon
   b. Jean Piaget
   c. Edward Titchener
   d. Wilhelm Wundt

7. If you were interested in exploring those thoughts, feelings, and emotions that lie outside one's awareness, you might be considered a student of _____ psychology.
   a. Gestalt
   b. psychoanalytic
   c. cognitive behavioral
   d. humanistic

8. The slogan "Be all that you can be" is an example of
   a. self-actualization.
   b. self-evaluation.
   c. self-concept.
   d. self-esteem.

9. _____ is best described as the study of human strengths, virtues, and optimal behavior.
   a. The psychological perspective
   b. The biological perspective
   c. Positive psychology
   d. The sociocultural perspective

10. Joshua works with children who demonstrate difficulties in successfully adjusting to kindergarten. It is most probable that Joshua is a _____ psychologist.
    a. clinical
    b. counseling
    c. psychoanalytic
    d. social

11. In an experiment on the effects of caffeine on college student test performance, caffeine would be considered the
    a. independent variable.
    b. dependent variable.
    c. extraneous variable.
    d. conditioned response.

12. Your friend visits a local mental health clinic where he receives psychotherapy and a prescription for an antidepressant. Your friend has probably seen a
    a. counselor.
    b. psychiatric social worker.
    c. psychiatrist.
    d. psychologist.

13. Issues such as competency levels and a client's right to confidentiality and privacy are examples of _____ standards or guidelines.
    a. ethical
    b. moral
    c. legal
    d. psychological

14. _____ means that a participant has an equal chance of being in either the experimental group or the control group.
    a. Placebo effect
    b. Self-fulfilling prophecy
    c. Random assignment
    d. Representative sampling

15. If you are approached at the mall and answer questions regarding your buying preferences, you have probably just participated in a(n)
    a. naturalistic observation.
    b. survey.
    c. experiment.
    d. correlational study.

16. Dr. Walinski is attempting to prove a cause-and-effect relationship between the viewing of violent media and subsequent increases in aggressive behaviors. The research method he will most likely utilize in this attempt would be a(n)
    a. experiment.
    b. survey.
    c. clinical study.
    d. random sample.

17. In an attempt to reduce the _____, you install cameras to covertly record the behaviors of students who are riding on the school bus.
    a. observer bias
    b. anthropomorphic error
    c. experimenter effect
    d. placebo effect

18. Which of the following correlation coefficients indicates the strongest relationship between two variables?
    a. 20.75
    b. 0
    c. 10.64
    d. 10.23

19. While researching a topic on the Internet for your introductory psychology course, the text recommends that you do the following:
    a. Take into account the source of the information.
    b. Be skeptical.
    c. Both (a) and (b).
    d. Neither (a) nor (b).

20. A professor believes that most students who sit at the back of the classroom are unmotivated and apathetic towards their studies. This belief is confirmed at the end of the semester as the majority of the back-row students are given a below-average grade. This outcome could be due to which of the following?
    a. observer effect
    b. self-fulfilling prophecy
    c. double-blind approach
    d. None of the above.

MODULE 2.1

Neurons and the Nervous System

The nervous system is divided into two major systems, then subdivided into more sections, each with their corresponding duties and responsibilities.

Central Nervous System

The central nervous system (CNS) consists of
- The brain (the central "computer" of the nervous system)
- The spinal cord (connecting the brain to other parts of the body).

Peripheral Nervous System

The peripheral nervous system (PNS) carries information to and from the CNS.

Autonomic Nervous System

The autonomic nervous system (ANS) serves the
- Internal organs
- Glands of the body

Somatic Nervous System

The somatic nervous system (SNS) carries messages to and from
- Sense organs
- Skeletal muscles

Sympathetic Branch

Emergency system that prepares the body for *fight or flight*.

Parasympathetic Branch

- Quiets the body and returns it to low levels of arousal
- Keeps vital life processes at moderate levels

The Neuron and Its Parts

The neuron is the *basic nerve cell* of the nervous system.
- It carries and processes information throughout the nervous system.
- 100 billion neurons join to form neural networks in our brain.
- Neural networks produce intelligence and consciousness.

Dendrites
- Receive messages from other neurons

Soma (Cell Body)
- Receives messages
- Contains cell nucleus
- Sends nerve impulses

Axon
- Thin fiber
- Transmits nerve impulses (action potential)

Axon Terminals
- Send messages to other neurons through chemicals called *neurotransmitters*

Brain Research

Methods for Studying Brain Structures

Methods for Studying Brain Functions

CT Scan
X-rays from numerous angles form one image

MRI Scan
The body is placed in a magnetic field. The image is processed by computer, yielding a 3-D model of the brain. An MRI is more detailed than a CT scan.

Ablation and Deep Lesioning
Involves surgical removal or damage to brain parts.

ESB
Electrical stimulation of the brain.

EEG
Uses electrodes to record neural impulses.

PET Scan
Positron emission tomography produces great images of activity.

fMRI
Provides images of activity throughout the brain.

Hemispheres and Lobes of the Cerebral Cortex

The cerebrum can be subdivided into both association cortex areas and the four lobes of the cerebral cortex.

Cerebrum

Two large hemispheres (the cerebrum) cover the upper part of the brain. Generally, each side of the brain controls functions on the opposing side of the body.

Association Cortex
The *association cortex*, the larger portion of the cortex, combines and processes information from the senses.

Brain Damage
Damage to association cortex can result in loss of function such as *aphasia*, impaired ability to use language.

Lobes of Cerebral Cortex
Large sections of the cerebral cortex are subdivided into lobes. Lobes perform *specific functions*.

Occipital Lobes
The occipital lobes at the rear of the brain process primary *visual information*.

Temporal Lobes
The temporal lobes located low on each side of the brain process *auditory information and language.*

Parietal Lobes
The parietal lobes register *body sensations* including touch, temperature, pressure, and other somatic sensations.

Frontal Lobes
Higher mental abilities, reasoning, and planning take place in the frontal lobes.

Brain Damage
Damage depends on the specific brain lobe that was affected.

7

Subcortex and Endocrine System

The cerebrum is not the only area that controls behavior.

Subcortex

Life-sustaining functions are controlled by subcortex structures.

Forebrain
Includes cerebral cortex

- *Hypothalmus* controls basic motives such as sex, eating, drinking, and sleep, and links the brain to the endocrine system.
- *Thalamus* acts as a switching station for sensory messages.

Limbic System
Primitive core of the brain.
- *Amygdala* is the brain's fear and emotional system.
- *Hippocampus* helps form lasting memories.

Midbrain
Connector

Hindbrain
Controls vital life functions

Reticular Formation and RAS
- *Reticular formation* influences attention and reflexes and prioritizes messages throughout the brain.
- *Reticular activating system (RAS)* stimulates the cortex, keeping it active and alert.

Hindbrain
Controls vital life functions
- *Medulla* controls breathing, heart rate, swallowing, etc.
- *Pons* is involved in sleep/arousal.
- *Cerebellum* controls muscular coordination, muscle tone, and posture.

Endocrine System

Glands in the endocrine system disperse *hormones* throughout the body, where they affect internal activities and behaviors. Linked to brain through the *hypothalamus*.

Pituitary Gland
- Regulates growth by releasing *growth hormone*.
- "Master Gland" of the endocrine system.

Pineal Gland
Controls body rhythms and sleep cycles by releasing *melatonin*.

Thyroid Gland
Controls metabolism.

Adrenal Gland
- Releases catecholamines and corticoids involved in fight-or-flight responses and stress.
- Secondary source of sex hormones.

Psychology in Action:
Handedness—Are You Dexterous or Sinister?

Right-Handers

Left-Handers

Brain Dominance

Advantages

Brain Dominance

Advantages

97%
Left brain

Right-handed world

68%
Left brain

Superiority in art

3%
Right brain

Longer lifespan

19%
Right brain

Less lateralization

12%
Both sides

Less language loss
after brain injury

Better math skills

Notes

_____

_____

_____

_____

_____

_____

_____

_____

1. The processing of information occurs in our
   a. brain.
   b. spinal cord.
   c. peripheral nervous system.
   d. sympathetic nervous system.

2. The _____ gap is the microscopic space between two neurons.
   a. somatic
   b. axonic
   c. synaptic
   d. dendritic

3. _____ are chemicals that alter activity within neurons and carry messages from one neuron to another.
   a. Neuropeptides
   b. Neurotransmitters
   c. Neural regulators
   d. Neural receptors

4. Kelli suffers from multiple sclerosis. If we examine a neuron from her brain, we may find degeneration of her
   a. soma.
   b. axon terminals.
   c. nerves.
   d. myelin.

5. While watching a scary movie, Caleb hears a sudden and unexpected noise. It is probable that such a situation would activate his _____ system.
   a. central nervous
   b. sympathetic
   c. parasympathetic
   d. somatic nervous

6. Which imaging technique utilizes strong magnetic fields to identify structures of the brain and the functions they control?
   a. CT scan
   b. fMRI scan
   c. EEG
   d. PET scan

7. Identify (of those listed) the least intrusive technique for brain study.
   a. deep lesioning
   b. ablation
   c. EEG
   d. electrical stimulation

8. _____ are large bundles of axons and dendrites.
   a. Nerves
   b. Neurons
   c. Neurogenesis
   d. Neurotoxins

9. Although only 3 millimeters thick, the _____ contains 70% of the neurons for the central nervous system.
   a. cerebrum
   b. corpus callosum
   c. cerebral cortex
   d. white matter

10. Approximately 95% of all people use their left hemisphere for language. This is an example of
    a. spatial neglect.
    b. corticalization.
    c. cerebral development.
    d. hemispheric specialization.

11. Body sensations, such as pressure, temperature and touch, are processed predominantly in the _____ lobe.
    a. temporal
    b. parietal
    c. frontal
    d. occipital

12. Damage to the _____ could result in disruption of reflexes and vital life functions.
    a. pons
    b. medulla
    c. cerebellum
    d. prefrontal lobe

13. Laurie kept pinching her arm to keep herself from falling asleep while driving. In doing so, Laurie was arousing her cortex by way of the
    a. reticular activating system.
    b. endocrine system.
    c. parasympathetic nervous system.
    d. central nervous system.

14. Tyron threw his golf club after missing his putt. What part of his brain was involved in this expression of frustration and anger?
    a. limbic system
    b. endocrine system
    c. reticular formation
    d. Broca's region

15. Chemicals that are carried throughout the body, affecting both internal activities and visible behavior, are called
    a. neurotransmitters.
    b. neuropeptides.
    c. hormones.
    d. GABA.

16. _____ might be released in someone watching a scary movie, whereas getting angry at the person who is talking during the movie would instead result in the release of _____.
    a. Epinephrine; norepinephrine
    b. Norepinephrine; epinephrine
    c. Testosterone; melatonin
    d. Melatonin; testosterone

17. Whether one is right or left handed is influenced by
    a. genetics.
    b. social pressures.
    c. birth traumas.
    d. All of the above.

18. The specialization of abilities to the right or left hemispheres of the brain is referred to as
    a. plasticity.
    b. lateralization.
    c. neurogenesis.
    d. action potential.

19. What are the short, branchlike structures of a neuron that receive signals from receptors or other neurons?
    a. axons
    b. somas
    c. dendrites
    d. cell membranes

20. Which of these activities most likely involves activation of the parasympathetic division?
    a. reading a newspaper article about stress
    b. taking an introductory psychology practice test
    c. resting after a stressful meeting
    d. getting oneself motivated to go exercise

MODULE 3.1

The Interplay of Heredity and Environment
Nature or nurture?

Heredity (Nature)

What did you inherit from your parents?
Genetics
- Genetic transmission of physical and psychological characteristics
- Dominant or recessive
- Polygenic control

Examples:
- Eye color
- Genetic disorders, such as hemophilia, MS

Environment (Nurture)

How were you raised?
Environment
- External conditions that affect a person
- Prenatal influences
- Sensitive periods
- Enriched or deprived environments

Examples:
- Congenital problems
- Fetal alcohol syndrome
- Poverty

Both
Reciprocal Influences

Example:
Temperament (genetic)   Parent-child bond (nurture)

MODULE 3.2

The Neonate and Early Maturation
Infant reflexes

Grasping Reflex
Babies grasp tightly when an object is placed in their palms.

Rooting Reflex
Babies reflexively turn their heads when touched on the cheek.

Sucking Reflex
Babies reflexively suck to obtain food when touched on the lips.

Moro Reflex
Babies make a hugging motion when startled by a loud noise.

Notes

_____

_____

_____

_____

_____

_____

_____

_____

Social Development in Childhood

Attachment
The close emotional bond that babies form with their primary caregivers.

Secure Attachment
Children with secure attachment show stable and positive emotional bonds.
- They are upset by their mother's absence.
- They seek closeness upon her return.

Insecure Attachment

Avoidant
Children with avoidant attachment have anxious emotional bonds. They turn away from their mother upon return.

Ambivalent
Children with ambivalent attachment have anxious emotional bonds. They show mixed feelings: they seek closeness and resist contact.

Language Development in Childhood

Birth
Use crying to get attention

6-8 Weeks Old
Begin cooing, repeating vowels "oo" or "ah"

6-8 Months Old
Begin babbling, mixing consonants with vowels such as "dadadada" or "bababa"

1 Year Old
Begin responding to real words, say "Mama" or "Dada"

18 Months-2 Years Old
Use 100 words or more, first in single-word stage, then two-word stage: use telegraphic speech

Notes

_____

_____

_____

_____

_____

_____

_____

Cognitive Development in Childhood

Piaget's stages.

Sensorimotor Stage (0-2 Years)

- Involves motor and sensory coordination
- Object permanence emerges
- Child's conceptions become more stable

Preoperational Stage (2-7 Years)

- Symbolic thinking and language strengthen
- Child's thinking is very intuitive
- Child is egocentric

Concrete Operational Stage (7-11 Years)

- Conservation and reversibility emerge
- Child's thinking is more logical, yet very concrete

Formal Operations Stage (11 Years and Up)

- Abstract thinking emerges
- Metacognition emerges: thinking about thinking
- Full adult intellectual ability is attained
  - Inductive and deductive thought
  - Scientific thought
  - Knowledge, experience, and wisdom

Adolescence, Young Adulthood, and Moral Development

Kohlberg's Levels of Moral Development

Preconventional Level

Moral thinking guided by consequences of actions: punishment, rewards, or mutual benefit.

Conventional Level

Moral thinking guided by desire to please others or to follow accepted authority, rules, and values.

Postconventional Level

Moral thinking guided by self-chosen ethical principles that are general, comprehensive, and universal.

Notes

Challenges Across the Lifespan

Erikson's Stages of Psychosocial Dilemma

0-1 Year: Trust vs. Mistrust
Loved, touched, nurtured

1-3 Years: Autonomy vs. Shame and Doubt
Independence is encouraged

3-5 Years: Initiative vs. Guilt
Makes plans and is allowed to carry them out

6-12 Years: Industry vs. Inferiority
Able to succeed in school

Adolescence: Identity vs. Role Confusion
Able to build a stable identity

Young Adulthood: Intimacy vs. Isolation
Able to share meaningful relationships

Middle Adulthood: Generativity vs. Stagnation
Desires to guide the next generation

Late Adulthood: Integrity vs. Despair
Able to view life with acceptance and satisfaction

Psychology in Action: Effective Parenting—Raising Healthy Children

Power Assertion
Using physical punishment or a show of force, such as taking away toys or privileges

Associated with fear, hatred of parents, and a lack of spontaneity and warmth Child has *low self-esteem.*

Withdrawal of Love
Refusing to speak to a child, threatening to leave, rejecting the child, or otherwise acting as if the child is temporarily unlovable

Produces "model" children, yet they are often anxious, insecure, and dependent on adults for approval. Child has *low self-esteem.*

Child Management Techniques
- Combining praise, recognition, approval, rules, and reasoning to encourage desirable behavior.
- Parent uses communication that is fair but loving and authoritative yet sensitive. This allows the child to move freely within consistent, well-defined boundaries for acceptable behavior.
- Must be carefully adjusted to child's level of understanding, because younger children don't always see the connection between rules, explanations, and their own behavior.

Produces socialized children who love and trust their parents. Children feel free to express their deepest feelings. Children move freely within consistent, well-defined boundaries for acceptable behavior. Child has *high self-esteem.*

1. Developmental psychology is the study of progressive changes in behavior and abilities in an individual, from _____ to death.
   a. birth
   b. conception
   c. infancy
   d. childhood

2. Dr. Worthington believes people who are intelligent have become so because of their life experiences. Dr. Jakway believes people are more or less intelligent because of genetic factors. What developmental psychology debate is illustrated by their disagreement?
   a. nature versus nurture
   b. correlation versus causation
   c. psychology versus philosophy
   d. cognitive psychology versus biological psychology

3. The typical human cell (excluding sex cells) contains how many chromosomes?
   a. 46 pairs
   b. 23
   c. 46
   d. Each cell has a varying number of chromosomes.

4. A trait controlled by a dominant gene
   a. will be expressed even if the instructions of the corresponding gene in the other half of the pair are different.
   b. may or may not be expressed, depending upon whether environmental conditions facilitate or prevent the expression of the trait.
   c. is always a positive, beneficial trait.
   d. will be expressed only if the instructions of the corresponding gene in the other half of the pair are the same.

5. Anything capable of directly causing birth defects (like alcohol) is known as a
   a. congenital problem.
   b. genetic disorder.
   c. teratogen.
   d. sensitive period.

6. An infant's home would be considered _____ if it is deliberately made more stimulating.
   a. beneficial
   b. detrimental
   c. depressing
   d. enriching

7. Core is to apple as _____ is to personality.
   a. reaction range
   b. temperament
   c. reciprocal series
   d. environment

8. _____ determines one's developmental level.
   a. Heredity
   b. Environment
   c. Behavior
   d. All of the above.

9. Which of the following is not one of the three categories for temperament?
   a. slow to warm up
   b. disorganized
   c. difficult
   d. easy

10. How might you elicit the grasping reflex in a neonate?
    a. Stroke his or her cheek lightly.
    b. Place a bottle in the child's mouth.
    c. Loudly clap your hands.
    d. Place your finger in the palm of the neonate's hand.

11. The physical growth and development of the body, brain, and nervous system is known as
    a. maturation.
    b. cephalocaudal development.
    c. proximodistal development.
    d. augmentation.

12. As discussed in the text regarding human development, although _____ may vary, _____ will typically remain the same.
    a. order; rate
    b. intelligence; motor skills
    c. rate; order
    d. motor skills; intelligence

13. At 10 months of age, Elizabeth displays mild anxiety when her mother leaves the room. This may be a direct sign that _____ has occurred.
    a. social referencing
    b. social development
    c. an insecure attachment
    d. a secure attachment

14. Which Baumrind parenting style utilizes high levels of firm and consistent guidance along with increased amounts of warmth and love?
    a. authoritarian
    b. authoritative
    c. overly permissive
    d. None of the above.

15. While talking to his infant daughter, Doug raises his voice and begins to speak in short, simple sentences. His change in speech is known as an example of
    a. receptive language.
    b. expressive language.
    c. parentese.
    d. infant inflections.

16. _____ is the culturally defined period between childhood and adulthood.
    a. Puberty
    b. Adolescence
    c. Young adulthood
    d. Child-adult transition

17. Your niece sees an airplane flying overhead and states, "Look at the birdie!" This is an example of Piagetian process of
    a. assimilation.
    b. accommodation.
    c. inductive thought.
    d. deductive thought.

18. Mary Ainsworth identified all of the following classifications of attachment except
    a. securely attached.
    b. insecure-deteriorated.
    c. insecure-avoidant.
    d. insecure-ambivalent.

19. Dennis states that during emergencies, he believes it is "OK" to speed. His identification of this self-chosen moral principle may be considered an example of moral reasoning at the
    a. preconventional level.
    b. conventional level.
    c. postconventional level.
    d. concrete level.

20. What factor is generally considered to be an essential aspect of an infant's first psychosocial task (Erikson)?
    a. learning to control body sensations or developing shame if unsuccessful and not sensitively treated by caregivers
    b. becoming aware of pleasurable sensations and sharing these sensations with others
    c. receiving encouragement, guidance, and reinforcement from caregivers and developing a sense of independence or autonomy
    d. being treated lovingly and predictably by caregivers and learning to trust

Chapter 4

Sensation and Perception

Sensory Systems and Selective Attention

Data Reduction
Through psychophysics, physical energy is measured and related to dimensions of the resulting sensations.

Sensory Adaptation
Sensory receptors respond less to unchanging stimuli.

Sensory Analysis
Sensory information is divided by perceptual features.

Sensory Coding
Sensory information is converted into neural messages understood by the brain.

Vision
How do we see?

Normal Vision
Various wavelengths of light make up the visible spectrum.

Short Wavelengths
- 400 nanometers
- Purple or violet sensations

Long Wavelengths
- 700 nanometers
- Blue, green, yellow, orange, and red

Visual Problems
- The shape of the eye affects the ability to focus:
- Hyperopia (farsightedness)
- Myopia (nearsightedness)
- Astigmatism (multiple focal points)
- Presbyopia (farsightedness due to aging)
- The sensitivity of the eye affects the ability to produce color sensation; color blindness

Eye Structure
The eye is like a camera relying on a lens and light receptors.

Cornea
Clear membrane that bends light inward

Lens
Focuses images on the retina

Retina
Has a layer of photoreceptors

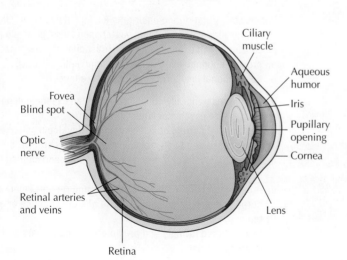

Ciliary muscle
Aqueous humor
Iris
Pupillary opening
Cornea
Lens
Fovea
Blind spot
Optic nerve
Retinal arteries and veins
Retina

Hearing, the Chemical Senses, and the Somesthetic Senses

Hearing, smell, and taste help keep us safe and add pleasure to our lives.

Hearing

A series of invisible waves of *compression* and *rarefaction* in the air provide the stimulus for sound.

How We Hear

1. First, the visible part of the ear concentrates sound waves and funnels them to the eardrum.
2. Second, a series of actions result in nerve impulses to the brain.

Deafness

Deafness comes in two main forms:
1. *Conduction deafness* happens when sounds are carried ineffectively from eardrum to inner ear.
2. *Nerve deafness* involves damage to the hair cells or the auditory nerve.

The Chemical Senses: Smell and Taste

Olfaction (smell) and gustation (taste) are responsive to chemical molecules.

Smell

At least 10,000 different odors can be detected based on which receptors are activated and where they are located.

The number of activated cells indicates how strong an odor is.

Taste and Flavors

Four (possibly five) basic tastes combine with sensations of texture, temperature, smell, and pain to provide us the many different flavors.

Perceptual Constancies and Perceptual Grouping

Perceptual constancies help us to interpret sensory information that is constantly changing.

Size Constancy

The perceived size of an object remains stable, even though the size of its retinal image changes.

Shape Constancy

The perceived shape of an object remains stable, even though the shape of its retinal image changes.

Brightness Constancy

Brightness of an object appears stable even though the lighting conditions change.

Depth Perception

The ability to see three-dimensional space and judge distances is vital to many daily functions.

Binocular Cues

Convergence
When looking at something that is 50 feet or less in distance, the eyes must turn in (converge) to focus on the object.

Retinal Disparity
Because the eyes are spaced 2.5 inches apart, each eye receives a slightly different view of the world.

Monocular Cues

Accommodation
When looking at something within 4 feet of each eye, the lens bends in order to focus on nearby objects.

Pictorial Cues
We perceive depth on two-dimensional surfaces such as paintings and photos by use of pictorial cues:
- Linear perspective
- Relative size
- Height in picture plane
- Light and shadow
- Overlap
- Texture gradients
- Aerial perspective
- Relative motion

Perception and Objectivity

Learning, expectations, and motives can alter our perception of the world.

Perceptual Learning
Learning can affect how we process sensory information. We may learn to focus on just one part of a group of stimuli.

Perceptual Habits
Learning may create ingrained patterns of organization and attention (perceptual habits).

Illusions
Illusions are distorted perceptions of stimuli that actually exist. Perceptual learning contributes to illusions.

Lack of Objectivity
Perception is not always objective. A variety of factors may influence what we perceive.

Attention
Attention is key to perception. Failure to pay attention to stimuli can result in not perceiving important events.

Motives and Attention
Your motives may make you focus on, or ignore, stimuli.

Hallucinations
Hallucinations are sensory (sight, sound, smell, taste, or touch) perceptions that have no external reality.

Perceptual Expectancies
Expectancies prepare you to perceive what you expect to perceive. Suggestion may play a large part in expectancies.

Extrasensory Perception

The purported ability to perceive events in ways outside the normal senses is a topic that fascinates many people.

Telepathy
The ability to read someone else's mind.

Clairvoyance
The ability to perceive events or information without regard to distance or physical barriers.

Precognition
The ability to perceive or predict future events.

Psychokinesis
The ability to influence inanimate objects by willpower.

Psychology in Action: Becoming a Better Eyewitness to Life

Tips for becoming a better eyewitness to life.

Remember that perceptions are constructions of reality.

Break perceptual habits and interrupt habituation.

Shift adaptation levels and broaden frames of reference by seeking out-of-the-ordinary experiences.

Beware of perceptual sets.

Be aware of the ways in which motives and emotions influence perceptions.

Make a habit of engaging in reality testing.

Pay attention.

1. You turn on the radio in your car; however, it is turned down so low that you cannot hear it. Someone utilizing the approach of psychophysics would say that the sound had not reached
   a. minimum threshold.
   b. absolute threshold.
   c. sensory adaptation.
   d. sensory identification.

2. You answer your phone and immediately recognize the voice of your best friend. What process is involved in this recognition?
   a. olfaction
   b. perception
   c. adaptation
   d. sensation

3. The cornea, or the lens, of Josh's eye is misshapen, resulting in part of his vision being focused and part being fuzzy. This problem is commonly referred to as
   a. hyperopia.
   b. myopia.
   c. presbyopia.
   d. astigmatism.

4. The physical height of a sound wave corresponds to what we would typically refer to as
   a. frequency.
   b. loudness.
   c. pitch.
   d. range.

5. As you move from a darkened movie theater into the bright theater lobby, your eye transitions from using its _____ to _____.
   a. cones; rods
   b. photo receptors; bars
   c. rods; cones
   d. cones; visual receptors

6. What type of hearing loss cannot be compensated for with the use of a hearing aid?
   a. conductive hearing loss
   b. innate hearing loss
   c. sensorineural hearing loss
   d. natural hearing loss

7. After reading information about the sense of taste, your friend asks you, "How, if there are only (up to) five different tastes that can be sensed, can there be so many flavors?" You correctly respond that
   a. additional information like texture and smell enhances taste.
   b. there are actually more than five tastes.
   c. the gustatory cortex fills in any missing information, resulting in additional flavors being perceived.
   d. None of the above.

8. What are the five taste sensations described in your text?
   a. rich, sweet, salty, bitter, sour
   b. bitter, sweet, hot, cool, salty
   c. brothy, buttery, sweet, sour, bitter
   d. sweet, salty, sour, bitter, umami

9. Gustation and olfaction are similar in that they both
   a. require the sensing of chemicals.
   b. would be hard to live without.
   c. involve perception but not sensation.
   d. All of the above.

10. Receptors in muscles and joints that detect body position and movement are referred to as the _____ sense.
    a. gustatory
    b. kinesthetic
    c. vestibular
    d. lock and key

11. Which of the following statements about depth perception are true?
    a. It may develop as early as 2 weeks of age.
    b. It is, at a basic level, inborn.
    c. It is partly learned through experience.
    d. All of the above.

12. Analyzing information starting with small features and building upward to a complete perception is known as
    a. top-down processing.
    b. lateral processing.
    c. bottom-up processing.
    d. puzzle theory processing.

13. After you watch a horror movie, you begin to notice sounds both inside and outside the house that seem to be unusual. This change in perception may be due to what your text refers to as a perceptual
    a. disturbance.
    b. expectancy.
    c. sensory experience.
    d. hallucination.

14. An illusion
    a. is the same as a hallucination.
    b. typically accompanies many mental illnesses.
    c. is a perceptual misjudgment.
    d. is the perception of a sensation without the presence of any external energy.

15. The four basic forms of ESP include all of the following except
    a. clairvoyance.
    b. telepathy.
    c. psychokinesis.
    d. psychosurgery.

16. _____ is the decreased response to unchanging and predictable stimuli.
    a. Habituation
    b. Dishabituation
    c. Perceptual deprivation
    d. Sensory illusion

17. According to the text, all of the following could improve one's ability to be a better eyewitness except
    a. breaking perceptual habits and interrupting habituation.
    b. learning to regularly question your own perceptions.
    c. regularly testing reality.
    d. being wary of looking at facial expressions or making eye contact with others.

18. What is the theory of color vision based on three cone types: red, green, and blue?
    a. trichromatic theory
    b. opponent-process theory
    c. cone-color theory
    d. primary color theory

19. _____ explains motion sickness that one might experience as the result of a mismatch between information from vision (playing a video game in which you are riding a roller-coaster) and the vestibular system and kinesthetic senses (actually sitting still).
    a. Gate control theory
    b. Sensory conflict theory
    c. Lock and key theory
    d. Perceptual divergence theory

20. Voluntarily focusing on one thing while excluding other sensory messages is an example of
    a. selective attention.
    b. alternating concentration.
    c. discriminating awareness.
    d. selective exclusion.

Altered States and Sleep

Changes in the *quality* and *pattern* of mental activity are known as altered states of consciousness (ASC).

Consciousness

Consciousness consists of all the sensations, perceptions, memories, and feelings you are aware of at any instant.

Altered States of Consciousness

Changes occur in the *quality* and *pattern* of mental activity.

Waking Consciousness

A state of clear and organized alertness.

Sleep

Sleep is an innate biological rhythm that can never be entirely ignored.

Other Altered States

Examples include: drug-induced altered states, long-distance running, listening to music, meditation, hypnosis.

Stages of Sleep

As we sleep, we cycle in and out of four NREM sleep stages + REM

Stage 1 NREM: *Light sleep*–heart rate slows, breathing becomes irregular, muscles relax; EEG shows small, irregular waves

Stage 2 NREM: Sleep deepens, body temperature drops; EEG shows *sleep spindles*

Stage 3 NREM: New large and slow brain waves appear; EEG begins to show *delta waves*

Stage 4 NREM: *Deep sleep*–reached within 1 hour; EEG shows almost pure *delta waves*

REM: Rapid eye movement sleep is associated with dreaming.

Sleep Needs and Patterns

Individuals have varying needs for sleep. Averages range from 5 hours to 11 hours.

Sleep Deprivation

Going without sleep can result in:

· Hallucinations (and other reality distortions)
· Inability to perform required tasks
· Poor moods
· Accidents

Sleep Disturbances and Dreaming

Sleep disturbances are a serious risk to health and happiness. Sleep clinics treat thousands of people each year for sleep disorders or complaints.

Common Sleep Problems

Many factors contribute to our poor sleep quality in North America. Sleep problems are nearing epidemic rates. Thousands of people each year suffer from sleep disorders.

Insomnia
- Difficulty sleeping
- Frequent nighttime awakenings
- Waking too early
- Affects work, health, and relationships

Sleepwalking and Sleeptalking
- Usually take place during stage 3 and stage 4 sleep
- Somnabulists do many activities
- Sleeptalkers may not make sense

Nightmares and Night Terrors
- Nightmares are bad dreams (REM)
- Night terrors cause total panic, hallucinations, and high physiological arousal (NREM)

Narcolepsy
- Sudden irresistible sleep attacks
- May last a few minutes to 1/2 hour
- Victim sleeps while standing, talking, or even driving

Sleep Apnea
- Breathing stops for periods of 20 seconds to 2 minutes
- Causes the person to gulp for air

Sudden Infant Death Syndrome (SIDS)
- Also known as "crib death"
- Affects 1 of 500 babies per year
- Baby stops breathing after apnea

Dreams

Most people dream four or five times a night. Dreams are not always remembered.

REM Sleep Revisited
REM sleep is associated with normal dreaming. In children, REM may stimulate the developing brain. In adults, REM may prevent sensory deprivation and help to process emotional events.

Activation-Synthesis Hypothesis
The activation-synthesis hypothesis argues that several parts of the brain are activated during REM sleep, and the cortex of the brain synthesizes this activity into stories and visual images.

Dream Theories
Most theorists agree that dreams reflect our waking thoughts, fantasies, and emotions.

Psychodynamic Dream Theory
Freud's psychodynamic dream theory emphasized internal conflicts and unconscious forces disguised as dream symbols.

Hypnosis, Meditation, and Sensory Deprivation

Other altered states of consciousness (ASCs) play a role in human behavior.

Hypnosis

People are hypnotized by many different methods that encourage *focused attention, relaxation, easy acceptance* of suggestions, and use of *vivid imagination*.

Meditation

In general, meditation focuses attention and interrupts the typical flow of thoughts, worries, and analysis. Benefits include lower heart rate, blood pressure, muscle tension, and other signs of stress.

Sensory Deprivation

Limited or monotonous stimulation may produce bizarre sensations, distorted perceptions, and dangerous lapses in attention. Under proper conditions, sensory deprivation may help break long-standing habits.

MODULE 5.4

Psychoactive Drugs

Psychoactive drugs affect attention, judgment, memory, time sense, self-control, emotion, or perception.

Effects on the Brain

Drugs may imitate or alter neurotransmitters.
- Some drugs increase neurotransmission (stimulants).
- Other drugs slow or block stimulation (depressants).

Addiction

Addictive drugs stimulate the brain's reward circuitry.

Stimulants
("Uppers")
- Amphetamines
- Cocaine
- Caffeine
- Nicotine

Depressants
("Downers")
- Barbiturales
- GHB
- Tranquilizers
- Alcohol

Hallucinogens
- Marijuana
- Hashish
- LSD
- PCP

Physical Dependence
Physical dependence (addiction) exists when a person compulsively uses a drug to maintain bodily comfort.

Withdrawal Symptoms
When physical illness follows removal of a drug

Drug Tolerance
Reduced response to a drug

Psychological Dependence
Persons who develop a psychological dependence feel that a drug is necessary to maintain feelings of comfort or well-being.

Psychology in Action: Exploring and Using Dreams

Freud identified four dream processes, or mental filters, that disguise the meanings of dreams.

Condensation
Combines several people, objects, or events into a single dream image.

Displacement
May cause important emotions or actions of a dream to be redirected toward safe or seemingly unimportant images.

Symbolization
Dreams are often expressed in images that are symbolic rather than literal.

Secondary Elaboration
The tendency to make a dream more logical and to add details when remembering it.

Notes

_____

_____

_____

_____

_____

_____

_____

1. Psychologists refer to _____ as all the sensations, perceptions, memories, and feelings that you are aware of at any given moment.
   a. unconscious
   b. preconscience
   c. conscience
   d. consciousness

2. All of the following would be considered altered states of consciousness except
   a. sleep.
   b. severe states of dehydration.
   c. intoxication.
   d. watching your favorite football team play in the Super Bowl.

3. REM sleep refers to
   a. sleep periods in which a person's eyes move rapidly.
   b. sleep periods ranging from stage 1 to stage 4.
   c. sleep periods in which night terrors might occur.
   d. sleep periods in which only 10% of all dreaming occurs.

4. A _____ is a brief shift in brain activity to the pattern normally recorded during sleep.
   a. microsleep
   b. deprivation
   c. hypersomnia
   d. daydream

5. Tony is experiencing sleep deprivation. Due to this deprivation, Tony may
   a. experience sensory illusions or hallucinations.
   b. have trouble paying attention to routine activities.
   c. be at greater risk for being in a car accident.
   d. All of the above.

6. While you are awake, an EEG registers _____ waves in your brain. However, while you are asleep your brain produces _____ waves.
   a. alpha; beta
   b. beta; alpha
   c. alpha; delta
   d. delta; alpha

7. Just as you are drifting off to sleep the muscles in your leg twitch, causing you to wake up. This twitch is referred to as a
   a. hypnic jerk.
   b. sleep spindle.
   c. stage 1 spasm.
   d. dream shudder.

8. Insomnia includes
   a. trouble falling asleep.
   b. trouble staying asleep.
   c. waking up to early.
   d. All of the above.

9. In order to try to sleep, you instead try to keep your eyes open as long as possible. This behavioral remedy for insomnia is referred to as
   a. systematic relaxation.
   b. paradoxical intention.
   c. stimulus control.
   d. sleep contradiction.

10. Nightmare is to night terror as:
    a. REM is to NREM.
    b. bad is to worse.
    c. awake is to asleep.
    d. narcolepsy is to cataplexy.

11. An individual who suffers from sleep apnea will experience
    a. interrupted breathing while asleep.
    b. recurrent nightmares.
    c. increased REM sleep.
    d. reduced sleepiness during the day.

12. SIDS
    a. is seen in babies with a strong arousal reflex.
    b. is an acronym for serious inhalation deficit syndrome.
    c. annually affects approximately 1 out of every 500 babies.
    d. is less likely to affect babies who are open-mouth breathers.

13. _____ is defined by your text as an altered state of consciousness, characterized by narrowed attention and an increased openness to suggestion.
    a. Meditation
    b. Hypnosis
    c. Auto suggestion
    d. Dissociation

14. If you focus on the golf ball intently while taking exactly two practice swings before teeing off, you may be engaging in
    a. concentrative meditation.
    b. auto suggestion.
    c. mindfulness meditation.
    d. the use of a mantra.

15. Which of the following often characterize(s) addiction?
    a. drug withdrawal
    b. drug discomfort
    c. drug tolerance
    d. Both a and c.

16. Which of the following is not one of Freud's four identified dream processes?
    a. condensation
    b. recitation
    c. symbolization
    d. displacement

17. Larry stated that when he dreams, he sometimes realizes that he is in fact dreaming and then decides to do extraordinary things such as flying like Superman. This awareness during dreaming is called a _____ dream.
    a. lucid
    b. logical
    c. coherent
    d. cognent

18. Images in dreams that serve as visible signs of hidden ideas, desires, impulses, emotions, relationships, and so forth are called
    a. manifest images.
    b. latent symbols.
    c. dream images.
    d. dream symbols.

19. Which of the following is considered a depressant?
    a. cocaine
    b. alcohol
    c. caffeine
    d. nicotine

20. _____ is defined as downing five or more drinks (four for women) in a short time.
    a. Alcoholism
    b. Binge drinking
    c. Intoxication
    d. Alcohol dependence

MODULE 6.1

Learning and Classical Conditioning

Psychology is the scientific study of behavior and mental processes. Psychologists seek empirical evidence based on scientific observation.

Various Types of Learning

Learning is a relatively permanent change in behavior due to experience. Learning can result from classical, operant, or observational conditioning.

Classical Conditioning

- Classical conditioning is based on what happens before a response is made (antecedents).
- It involves passive behaviors.
- A neutral stimulus (NS) is paired repeatedly with an unconditioned stimulus (US) (unlearned) that leads to an unconditioned response (UR).
- Learning happens when the neutral stimulus is able to elicit the same response, now called the conditioned response (CR).

Operant Conditioning

- Operant conditioning is based on what happens after a response is made (consequences).
- It involves active behaviors as the learner operates on the environment.
- A response is made that is followed by either a reinforcing or punishing consequence.
- Learning happens when an event that follows a response increases the probability of repetition of the response.

Generalization

After conditioning, a stimulus that is similar to the original NS may cause the conditioned response.

Discrimination

Stimulus discrimination occurs when similar stimuli evoke different responses.

Extinction and Spontaneous Recovery

- Removing the US causes the CR to cease (extinction of the response).
- The CR may reappear in response to a generalized stimulus (spontaneous recovery of the response).

Conditioned Emotional Responses

- Conditioned responses may not be just reflexes.
- Responses may be emotional.
- Phobias (learned fears) are conditioned emotional responses (CERs).

Vicarious Conditioning

- Observing what happens to others may cause a conditioned response (vicarious classical conditioning).
- Vicarious conditioning involves learning from watching the reinforcement or punishment of others.

Operant Conditioning

Behaviors and consequences play a role in operant conditioning. Responses are voluntary (unlike classical conditioning) because we learn to expect that a certain response will lead to a certain effect (consequence). Consequences can be either reinforcing or punishing.

Reinforcement

An operant reinforcer is a consequence that *increases* the chance that the behavior will be repeated.

Positive Reinforcement
- Occurs when a response leads to the addition of a pleasant or desirable consequence.
- Increases responses.

Negative Reinforcement
- Occurs when a response leads to the removal of an unpleasant or undesirable event.
- Like positive reinforcement, negative reinforcement increases responses.

Punishment

Punishment is an aversive consequence that *decreases* the chance that the behavior will be repeated.

Punishment by Application
- Occurs when a response leads to the addition of an unpleasant or undesirable consequence.
- Decreases responses.

Punishment by Removal
- Occurs when a response leads to the removal of a pleasant or desirable event (negative reinforcement).
- Like punishment by application, it decreases responses.

Partial Reinforcement and Stimulus Control

Schedules of Partial Reinforcement

Partial reinforcement can be given in a variety of patterns. Reinforcement patterns can be either based on ratios or intervals.

Ratio Schedules
Based on number of responses

Interval Schedules
Based on time elapsed

Fixed Ratio (FR)
Reinforcement is given after a set number of responses. FR produces high response rates.

Variable Ratio (VR)
Reinforcement is given after a varied number of responses. VR is highly resistant to extinction.

Fixed Interval (FI)
Reinforcement is given after a fixed amount of time has elapsed between correct responses. The number of responses makes no difference in reinforcement.

Variable Interval (VI)
Reinforcement is given after a varied amount of time has passed between responses. Slow, steady response rates are produced.

Punishment

Punishment is frequently used to control behavior.

Variables Affecting Punishment

Behaviors are performed because there is some expectancy of reinforcement. The task of punishment is to overcome the reinforcement value.

Timing

Punishment should be given as the response is made or immediately after the response. This allows the learner to associate the behavior to the consequence.

Consistency

Punishment should be given each time an undesirable behavior occurs. Partially punishing a behavior will not speed extinction.

Intensity

Severe punishment may stop a behavior immediately and forever. The danger is in being too severe. Mild punishments may only have a temporary effect.

Side Effects of Punishment

As punishment increases in severity, so do the drawbacks.

Aversive

Punishment is painful or uncomfortable. Through classical conditioning, it can cause fear or resentment toward the person doing the punishing.

Escape and Avoidance

It is natural to try to avoid an aversive stimulus. Children may avoid parents and/or lie to parents to escape punishment.

Aggression

Aggression is a common response to frustration. Punishment can be very frustrating.

Cognitive Learning and Imitation

Using Punishment Wisely

Punishment should not be used at all when other means to discourage behavior are available. Positive reinforcement for not misbehaving is more effective than punishment.

Apply punishment during, or immediately after, misbehavior.

Be consistent.

Use the minimum punishment necessary to suppress behavior.

Avoid harsh punishment.

Don't rely exclusively on punishment.

Expect anger from a punished person.

Punish with kindness and respect.

Cognitive Learning

Learning that involves higher mental processes, such as memory, thinking, problem solving, understanding, knowing, and anticipating.

Latent Learning

Learning remains hidden or unseen until a reward or incentive for performance is offered.

Discovery Learning

Learning emphasizes insight and understanding, in contrast to rote learning.

Observational Learning

Learning is influenced by observing and imitating the actions of another person or learning from the consequences of their actions.

Psychology in Action: Behavioral Self-Management—A Rewarding Project

By applying learning principles to one's life, many behaviors can be improved.

Applying Operant Conditioning

By applying operant conditioning principles, it is possible to change or manage your own behavior.

1. Choose a Target Behavior
Identify the activity you want to change.

2. Record a Baseline
Record how much time you currently spend performing the target activity or count the number of desired or undesired responses you make each day.

3. Establish Goals
Remember the principle of shaping, and set realistic goals for gradual improvement on each successive week. Also, set daily goals that add up to the weekly goal.

4. Choose Reinforcers
Establish daily and weekly rewards for your accomplishments.

5. Record Your Progress
Keep accurate records of the amount of time spend each day on the desired activity or the number of times you make the desired response.

6. Reward Successes
If you meet your daily goal, collect your reward. If you fall short, be honest with yourself and skip the reward. Do the same for weekly goals.

7. Adjust Your Plan as You Learn More About Your Behavior
Overall progress will reinforce your attempts at self-management.

Breaking Bad Habits

Here are additional strategies that can help break bad habits.

Reinforce Alternative Responses
Try to get the same reinforcement with a new response.

Promote Extinction
Try to discover what is reinforcing an unwanted response and remove, avoid, or delay the reinforcement.

Break Response Chains
Break up response chains that precede an undesired behavior. Scramble the chain of events that leads to an undesired response.

Avoid Antecedent Cues
Try to avoid, narrow down, or remove stimuli that elicit the bad habit.

Try Behavioral Contracting
If all else fails, try behavioral contracting.
- First, state the specific problem behavior you want to control, or a goal you want to achieve.
- Second, state the rewards you will receive, privileges you will forfeit, or punishments you must accept.
- Third, sign the contract and have a person you trust also sign.
- Follow through.

1. Which term describes a relatively permanent change in behavior or the potential to make a response that occurs as a result of experience?
   a. learning
   b. conditioning
   c. perception
   d. understanding

2. Caleb gets paid $5 each week for mowing the lawn. If the money Caleb gets paid each week makes it more likely that he will mow the lawn again the following week, behavioral psychologists would refer to the money as a(n)
   a. allowance.
   b. bribe.
   c. reward.
   d. reinforcement.

3. Events that precede an experience are called _____, whereas those that follow a response are known as _____.
   a. punishments; reinforcements
   b. consequences; antecedents
   c. reinforcements; punishments
   d. antecedents; consequences

4. What must be paired together for classical conditioning to occur?
   a. neutral stimulus and conditioned stimulus
   b. neutral stimulus and unconditioned stimulus
   c. conditioned response and unconditioned response
   d. unconditioned stimulus and conditioned response

5. If you have the goal of teaching someone to respond reflexively to a stimulus that currently evokes no response, you will most likely utilize a(n) _____ approach.
   a. operant conditioning
   b. classical conditioning
   c. instrumental learning
   d. observational learning

6. While growing up, Susan often observed her mother have a panic attack in the presence of mice. As an adult, Susan now responds with intense anxiety at even the thought of a mouse. This learning of an emotional response would be considered an example of
   a. vicarious learning.
   b. indirect conditioning.
   c. instrumental conditioning.
   d. operant learning.

7. Stimulus _____ occurs when we learn to respond to a particular stimulus but not to others that are similar.
   a. identification
   b. extinction
   c. generalization
   d. discrimination

8. Edward L. Thorndike referred to the probability of a response being altered by the effect it has as
   a. classical conditioning.
   b. the theory of consequences.
   c. the law of effect.
   d. the state of affairs

9. The text describes operant reinforcement as being most effective when it _____ a correct response.
   a. rapidly follows
   b. rapidly precedes
   c. is delayed, following
   d. is prematurely given, preceding

10. Behaviors that are repeated because they appear to produce reinforcement (even though they are actually unrelated) are often referred to as _____ behaviors.
    a. correlational
    b. superstitious
    c. consequential
    d. substantial

11. The process of reinforcing successive approximations is called
    a. shaping.
    b. molding.
    c. cognitive mapping.
    d. delayed gratification.

12. One way to differentiate operant conditioning from classical conditioning is to decide if the
    a. response is voluntary or reflexive in nature.
    b. stimulus is conditioned or unconditioned.
    c. response is pleasant or unpleasant.
    d. antecedent comes before or after the response.

13. Giving a child a spanking is an example of
    a. a negative reinforcement.
    b. a punishment.
    c. an antecedent.
    d. vicarious learning.

14. Magnolia took an aspirin, which subsequently relieved her headache. This relief is an example of a
    a. punishment.
    b. positive reinforcement.
    c. stimulus generalization.
    d. negative reinforcement.

15. Cookies and a glass of milk would be considered a _____ reinforcer.
    a. secondary
    b. primary
    c. token
    d. social

16. Ty gets paid at his job every 2 weeks, whereas Jevon gets paid for every car he sells. Ty's schedule of reinforcement is _____, and Jevon's is _____.
    a. fixed interval; variable ratio
    b. fixed ratio; variable interval
    c. variable interval; variable ratio
    d. fixed interval; fixed ratio

17. The text describes all of the following drawbacks with punishment except
    a. avoidance learning.
    b. increased effectiveness in toilet training.
    c. escape learning.
    d. increasing aggression.

18. _____ refers to understanding, knowing, anticipating, or otherwise making use of information-rich higher mental processes.
    a. Observational learning
    b. Latent learning
    c. Cognitive learning
    d. Discovery learning

19. In creating your plan for how you will move through campus to get to your next class, it is likely you will use a
    a. cognitive route.
    b. created image.
    c. symbol representation.
    d. cognitive map.

20. Tracy was asked to label the keys on a blank computer keyboard. She initially stated that she would not be able to do it. However, upon being offered $50 if she could do it successfully, Tracy was able to complete the task. This is an example of _____ learning.
    a. passive
    b. manifest
    c. latent
    d. unintended

Chapter 7

Memory Systems

Psychologists have identified three stages of memory.

Sensory Memory

Sensory memory registers incoming information from the environment through our senses just long enough to move it to the next stage.

Iconic Memory

An exact copy of what you see (icon).

Echoic Memory

An exact copy of what you hear (echo).

Short-Term Memory

Holds small amounts of information in conscious awareness to be moved to the next stage.

Limited Capacity of Information

Holds ONLY small amounts of information.

Sensitive to Interruption and Interference

Difficult to do more than one task at a time.

Working Memory

Combines with other mental processes to "think."

Long-Term Memory

Acts as a lasting, nearly limitless, storehouse for knowledge. LTM is stored on basis of meaning and importance.

Unlimited Capacity of Information

Holds nearly limitless amounts of information.

Stored on the Basis of Meaning

New information must be linked to previous knowledge.

Notes

_____

_____

_____

_____

_____

_____

_____

_____

STM and LTM

Knowing the characteristics of STM and LTM can help make good use of your memory.

Short-Term Memory

STM *capacity* is typically about 7 bits of information (plus or minus 2). STM *duration* is typically about 12 to 18 seconds.

Chunking

By reorganizing information into *chunks* we can make better use of our short-term memory.

Rehearsal

Rehearsal (repetition) of information in STM stops it from being lost forever.

Maintenance Rehearsal

Lengthens the duration of STM.

Elaborative Rehearsal

Makes information more meaningful. Links new information to memories that are already in LTM.

Long-Term Memory

LTM acts as a lasting, nearly limitless storehouse of memory. LTM is stored on basis of meaning and importance.

Permanence

Experts believe that long-term memories are only relatively permanent.

Constructing Memories

Memories are often updated, changed, lost, or revised. These processes may result in including false information.

Organizing Memories

Information in LTM may be arranged hierarchically according to rules, images, categories, symbols, similarity, or meaning.

Redintegrative Memories

Redintegration occurs when entire past experiences are reconstructed from one small recollection.

Skill Memory and Fact Memory

Long-term memories fall into at least two categories: *procedural* (skill) memory and *declarative* (fact) memory.

Notes

_____

_____

_____

_____

_____

_____

_____

_____

Measuring Memory

Our memories may be revealed through various means.

Implicit and Explicit Memories

Memories from past experiences that are consciously brought to mind are *explicit*. Memories outside of awareness are *implicit*.

Explicit

Recall
A direct retrieval of facts or information involves *recall*.
Example: Essay exam

Recognition
In recognition memory, previously learned material is correctly identified.
Example: Multiple-choice exam

Relearning
Information learned once can be relearned with a "savings" in time or effort.

Implicit

Priming
Priming involves the activation of memories that lie outside of awareness.
Example: Riding a bike

Proactive
When prior learning inhibits recall of new learning.

Retroactive
When new learning inhibits recall of old learning.

Forgetting

Knowing how we "lose" memories helps us retain them. Why do we forget?

Encoding Failure
In many cases we "forget" because the memory was never formed (encoded) in the first place.

Repression
Through repression, memories are held out of consciousness.

Memory Decay
Memory traces (changes in nerve cells or brain activity) decay (fade) over time.

Suppression
Suppression is an active, conscious attempt to put something out of mind.

Cue-Dependent Forgetting
Memories may be "forgotten" because *memory cues* (stimuli associated with a memory) are missing.

State-Dependent Learning
The *bodily state* that exists during learning can be a strong cue for later memory. For example, if you learn a list of words while in a happy mood, you will recall those words better when you are happy again.

Interference
Interference refers to the tendency for new memories to impair retrieval of older memories (and the reverse).

Exceptional Memory and Improving Memory

Memory skills *can* be developed. The following are tips for building better memories.

Knowledge of Results
Feedback allows you to check your progress.

Selection
Memory chores will be more manageable if you select one or two important terms or ideas to focus on.

Recitation
Recitation (summarizing aloud) forces you to practice retrieving information.

Rehearsal
The more you mentally review (rehearse) information as you read, the better you will remember it.

Spaced Practice
Alternate short study sessions with brief rest periods.

Whole vs. Part Learning
The amount of material to be learned may dictate whether it is more efficiently leaned as a whole or in parts.

Organization
Difficult information can be organized into "chunks" for better retention.

Overlearning
Overlearning is the best insurance against going blank on a test.

Memory Cues
The best memory cues are the stimuli that were present during encoding.

Notes

_____

_____

_____

_____

_____

_____

_____

1. Memory includes all of the following processes except
   a. storage.
   b. encoding.
   c. bypassing.
   d. retrieving.

2. Which term describes a fleeting flurry of auditory activity that lasts for a few seconds or less?
   a. logo
   b. echo
   c. icon
   d. image

3. _____ attention is required in order to move information from sensory memory to short-term memory.
   a. Special
   b. Sustained
   c. Alternating
   d. Selective

4. In order for information to be stored for an extended period, it must pass into or through all of the following stages except
   a. sensory memory.
   b. short-term memory.
   c. long-term memory.
   d. episodic memory.

5. Most often, short-term memories are stored
   a. phonetically.
   b. mentally.
   c. with the sense of smell.
   d. as images.

6. Information that is transferred from short-term memory to long-term memory must either be _____ or _____.
   a. important; meaningful
   b. limited; general
   c. insightful; understood
   d. emphasized; memorized

7. _____ are made up of bits of information grouped into larger units.
   a. Information bits
   b. Rehearsing information
   c. Information chunks
   d. Information clusters

8. By repeating the phone number silently to himself, Shawn was able to prolong the memory. This is an example of
   a. chunking.
   b. episodic memory.
   c. elaborative memory.
   d. maintenance rehearsal.

9. When gaps in memory are filled in by logic, guessing, or new information, _____ has occurred.
   a. constructive processing
   b. elaborative memory
   c. confabulation
   d. redintegration

10. _____ is a technique created by Edward Geiselman and Ron Fisher and is used by law enforcement for jogging the memory of eyewitnesses and increasing the accuracy of the memories being recalled.
    a. Hypnosis
    b. Shaping
    c. Behavioral interview
    d. Cognitive interview

11. As you look through your old high school yearbook, you are flooded with memories. This process is known as
    a. redintegration.
    b. constructive processing.
    c. cognitive processing.
    d. memory networking.

12. Declarative memory can be divided into _____ and _____ memories.
    a. sensory; procedural
    b. short-term; long-term
    c. procedural; semantic
    d. semantic; episodic

13. _____ is the feeling that a memory is available, but not quite retrievable.
    a. Drew-a-blank
    b. Tip-of-the-tongue
    c. Feeling-of-knowing
    d. Interference

14. What do psychologists call it when you can remember the first and last items of your grocery list, but have problems with the items in the middle of the list?
    a. rote memory effect
    b. interference
    c. amnesia
    d. serial position effect

15. A memory that can be consciously brought to mind is referred to in the text as a(n)
    a. implicit memory.
    b. explicit memory.
    c. voluntary memory.
    d. intentional memory.

16. What did Ebbinghaus' curve of forgetting imply?
    a. Forgetting is slow at first and is then followed by a rapid decline.
    b. Forgetting is rapid at first and is then followed by a slow decline.
    c. Forgetting is a constant and does not change with time.
    d. Everyone forgets at different rates.

17. A multiple-choice question is a common test of
    a. identification.
    b. recall.
    c. recognition.
    d. detection.

18. Remembering where you where and what you were doing on the second Tuesday of September, 2001, only after being told it was September 11 (9/11), is an example of
    a. state-dependent learning.
    b. cue-dependent learning.
    c. recitation.
    d. date-dependent recall.

19. Suppression is to repression as _____ is to _____.
    a. unconscious; conscious
    b. recognition; recall
    c. conscious; unconscious
    d. recall; recognition

20. Following his car accident (in which he hit his head on the steering wheel), Jacob was unable to remember what he was doing *before* the accident. This gap in memory is an example of
    a. anterograde amnesia.
    b. proactive interference.
    c. retrograde amnesia.
    d. retroactive interference.

Chapter 8

MODULE 8.1

Intelligence

In general, intelligence is the global capacity to act purposefully, to think rationally, and to deal effectively with the environment.

Intelligence Tests

Stanford-Binet Intelligence Scales, 5th ed.
Provides a score for fluid reasoning, knowledge, quantitative reasoning, visual-spatial processing, and working memory.

Wechsler Scales
Provides a performance score (nonverbal) and a verbal score (language or symbol oriented).

Intelligence Quotients

Mental Age
Dividing *mental age* (the level a person answers age-related questions) by *chronological age* and multiplying by 100 gives an IQ.

Mental Giftedness
Individuals who score above 130 on IQ tests are often identified as "gifted." Gifted children typically (although not always) are successful as adults.

IQ and Environment
Most experts agree that improving social conditions and providing a stimulating environment can raise intelligence.

Deviation IQ
Measuring how high or how low a person scores *relative to his or her own age group* gives a different form of IQ.

Intellectual Disability
Mental abilities far below average are identified as *intellectually disabled*.

Causes of Intellectual Disability
Fetal damage, birth injuries, metabolic disorders, and genetic abnormalities may cause intellectual difficulties.

Notes

_____

_____

_____

_____

_____

_____

Imagery, Concepts, and Language

Cognition refers to mentally processing information. Abstract thinking is possible through *mental images, concepts,* and *language.*

Mental Images

Images are picture-like mental representations.
Most of us use images to think, remember, and solve problems.

Kinesthetic Imagery

Kinesthetic images are created from muscular sensations and help us think about movements and actions.

Concepts

Concepts are ideas that represent categories of objects or events.

Forming Concepts

Concept formation is the process of classifying the world into meaningful categories.

Meaning

Concepts have both
• an exact (denotative) meaning
• an emotional or personal (connotative) meaning.

Types of Concepts

Conjunctive concepts require two or more features.
Relational concepts are based on how an object relates to something else.
Disjunctive concepts have a least one of several possible features.

Language

Language consists of words or symbols and rules for combining them.

Structure of Language

Language requires:
1. *Grammar*—rules for making sounds into words and sentences
2. *Syntax*—rules for word order

Gestural Languages

Language is not limited to speech. Sign languages are true languages.

Look at  **Stare**

Problem Solving

Problem solving can be commonplace or highly significant.

Mechanical Solutions

Mechanical solutions are achieved by trial and error or by rote application of rules.

Least efficient.

Solutions by Understanding

Understanding (deep comprehension of a problem) is necessary in some cases.

Heuristics

Strategies for identifying and evaluating problem solutions (*heuristics*) typically involve a "rule of thumb" that reduces the number of alternatives to be considered.

More efficient.

Insightful Solutions

When understanding leads to a rapid solution, *insight* has taken place.

Nature of Insight

- *Selective encoding* is focusing on relevant information.
- *Selective combination* is bringing together apparently unrelated bits of useful information.
- *Selective comparison* is comparing new problems with old, solved problems which are the keys to insight.

Most efficient.

Barriers to Problem Solving

Common barriers to problem solving include:
- Functional fixedness
- Emotional barriers
- Cultural barriers
- Learned barriers
- Perceptual barriers

Notes

Creative Thinking and Intuition

Original ideas in art, medicine, music, and science have changed the course of human history.

Divergent vs. Convergent Thinking

Routine problem solving involves *convergent thinking*, which results in a single solution. Creative thinking involves *divergent thinking*, which results in multiple solutions.

Creative Thinking

Creative thinking involves:

- *Fluency* (number of suggestions made)
- *Flexibility* (number of times a shift is made to another set of possible solutions)
- *Originality* (how unusual an idea is)

Stages of Creative Thought

Five stages often seen in creative problem solving are:

- *Orientation*
- *Preparation*
- *Incubation*
- *Illumination*
- *Verification*

The Creative Personality

Thinking styles and personality characteristics have more to do with creativity than intelligence alone.

Creative Characteristics

Characteristics of creative thinking include:

- A wide range of knowledge and interests
- An openness to a variety of experiences
- Taking pleasure from symbolic thinking
- Independence
- A preference for complexity

Intuition

Intuition is quick, impulsive thought that lacks formal logic or clear reasoning.

Pitfalls of Intuition

Errors in intuitive thought include disregarding or *failing to recognize probability, emotional involvement,* and *how the problem is worded* (framed).

Psychology in Action: Culture, Race, IQ, and YOU

Cultural values, knowledge, language patterns, and traditions can greatly affect performance on tests designed for western cultures.

High-Stakes Testing

Widespread reliance on standardized testing raises questions about the relative good and harm that they do.

Positive Effects

1. Tests can open opportunities.
2. Test scores may be more fair and objective than subjective judgments made by individuals.
3. Test do accurately predict academic performance.

Culture-Fair Tests

Designed to minimize the importance of skills and knowledge that may be more common in some cultures than in others.

Negative Effects

1. Tests can close opportunities and exclude people of obvious ability.
2. Tests often contain poorly written or ambiguous questions.
3. Tests are often biased.
4. Most standardized tests do not test critical thinking, creativity, or problem solving.

Culture-Biased Tests

Fail to minimize the importance of skills and knowledge that may be more common in some cultures than in others.

1. _____ is the global capacity to act purposely, to think rationally, and to deal effectively with the environment.
   a. IQ
   b. Mental age
   c. Intelligence
   d. G factor

2. An operational definition of intelligence is based on
   a. the theoretical perspective of the clinician.
   b. the mental and psychological age of the person.
   c. the procedures used to measure intelligence.
   d. the general core of intelligence.

3. In order to estimate Sally's intelligence, we would need to know both her _____ and _____.
   a. mental age; test score
   b. developmental level; family history
   c. chronological age; mental age
   d. cultural background; emotional functioning

4. If an individual's chronological age is the same as his or her mental age, what would the IQ be?
   a. 100
   b. 125
   c. above average
   d. None of the above; more information is needed.

5. What do the Wechsler tests provide?
   a. verbal IQ
   b. full-scale IQ
   c. performance IQ
   d. All of the above.

6. In Gardner's theory of multiple intelligence, he identified all of the following types of intelligence except
   a. music.
   b. logic and math.
   c. interpersonal.
   d. common sense.

7. _____ usually refers to computer programs capable of doing things that require intelligence when done by people.
   a. Artificial intelligence
   b. Synthetic intelligence
   c. Cybernetics
   d. Software intellect

8. _____ refers to mentally processing information.
   a. Judgment
   b. Wisdom
   c. Cognition
   d. Maintenance rehearsal

9. The basic units of thought include all of the following except
   a. concepts.
   b. cognitions.
   c. languages.
   d. images.

10. Language allows events to be _____ into _____ for mental manipulation.
    a. encoded; symbols
    b. divided; parts
    c. separated; groupings
    d. programmed; neurons

11. Concept formation is based on experience with _____ and _____ instances.
    a. new; old
    b. created; stored
    c. familiar; novel
    d. positive; negative

12. A concept's _____ meaning is its exact or dictionary definition.
    a. faulty
    b. connotative
    c. denotative
    d. semantic

13. Doug attempted to find the correct key for the lock by using each key on the key ring. This is an example of a(n) _____ solution.
    a. understanding
    b. hypothetical
    c. functional
    d. mechanical

14. A(n) _____ is a "rule of thumb" that reduces the number of possible solutions.
    a. mnemonic
    b. algorithm
    c. heuristic
    d. general solution

15. Coach Ray explained that in order for the team to win, they simply needed to score more points than the other team. This is an example of a(n) _____ solution.
    a. functional
    b. general
    c. simple
    d. intentional

16. A sudden mental reorganization that makes the solution obvious is known as
    a. understanding.
    b. insight.
    c. enlightenment.
    d. perception.

17. If you are too inhibited to offer an answer in class because you are afraid of looking foolish, you may be experiencing a(n) _____ _____ barrier to problem solving.
    a. emotional
    b. cultural
    c. learned
    d. perceptual

18. You would be involved in _____ thinking if you were trying to come up with as many solutions as possible.
    a. convergent
    b. inductive
    c. divergent
    d. deductive

19. If Malika is attempting to gather all the pertinent information available in order to creatively solve a problem, we categorize her as being in the _____ stage.
    a. orientation
    b. preparation
    c. incubation
    d. verification

20. The text states that when we tend to give a choice greater weight if it seems to be representative of what we already know, we are experiencing
    a. the representativeness heuristic.
    b. intuition.
    c. functional fixedness.
    d. wisdom.

Chapter 9

Overview of Motivation

Motivation refers to the ways in which our actions are *initiated*, *sustained*, *directed*, and *terminated*.

A Model of Motivation

Needs (internal deficiencies) cause a *drive* (an energized motivational state), which prompts responses (an action or series of actions) to attain goals (the target of motivated behavior). Needs push. Behaviors can be activated by either needs or goals. Goals pull. There are three categories of motives:

Primary Motives

Primary motives are based on biological needs for food, water, air, etc. to ensure survival of the individual.

Homeostasis

An attempt to maintain a "steady state," a state of balance with regard to the primary motives, is referred to as *homeostasis*.

Stimulus Motives

Our needs for stimulation and information appear to be innate, but not strictly necessary for survival.

Examples:
- Activity
- Curiosity
- Exploration
- Manipulation
- Physical Contact

Secondary Motives

Secondary motives are based on *learned* needs, drives, and goals.

Examples:
- Power
- Affiliation
- Approval
- Status
- Security
- Achievement

Motivation and Emotion

Notes

Hunger, Thirst, Pain, and Sex

Hunger

Both internal and external factors direct hunger. The brain receives internal signals from the stomach, intestines, hormones, and liver. The brain also detects external eating cues, such as sight and availability of food.

Hypothalamus

Plays a critical role in determining if hunger begins and stops.

Set Point

The weight you maintain when you are making no effort to gain or lose weight.

Eating Disorders

Anorexia nervosa (self-starvation) and bulimia (excessive eating/purging) are health-, even life-threatening.

Diet

The *types* and *amounts* of food you regularly eat define your diet. Some diets encourage overeating.

Behavioral Dieting

Overhauling eating habits with an approach called *behavioral dieting* can assist weight loss.

Two Types of Thirst

1. Thirst develops when there is a loss of fluid volume *between* body cells (extracellular thirst).
2. Thirst develops when there is a loss of fluid from *within* body cells (intracellular thirst).

Pain

Pain is an episodic drive that prompts us to avoid damage to the body. Pain avoidance is at least partially learned.

Sex

Because sex is not necessary for *individual survival*, many psychologists do not consider it to be a true primary motive. It is *nonhomeostatic*.

Notes

_____

_____

_____

_____

_____

_____

Arousal, Achievement, and Growth Needs

Arousal: Stimulus Drives

Stimulus drives reflect our need for *information, exploration, manipulation*, and *sensory input*.

Arousal Theory

According to arousal theory, people attempt to maintain ideal levels of bodily arousal. We seek excitement or quiet when levels are too high or too low.

Sensation Seekers

People's needs for stimulation vary. Sensation seeking is a trait of people who prefer high levels of stimulation.

Achievement: Learned Motives

Social *(learned)* motives are acquired as part of growing up in a society or culture.

Need for Achievement

A need for achievement (nAch) is a desire to meet an internal standard of excellence.

Characteristics of Achievers

People with high nAch are moderate risk takers. They avoid goals that are too difficult or too easy.

Power

A need for power is a desire to have impact or control over others.

Growth: Growth Needs

Maslow's hierarchy of human needs places growth needs (self-actualization) at the top.

Intrinsic and Extrinsic Motivation

To act without any obvious external rewards is to be *intrinsically motivated*. When obvious external factors prompt our action, we are *extrinsically* motivated.

Creativity

People are more likely to be creative when they are intrinsically motivated.

Notes

_____

_____

_____

_____

_____

_____

_____

Emotion and Physiological Arousal

Emotion is characterized by *physiological arousal*, *subjective feelings* (private, internal experience), and *changes in behavior* (facial expressions, gestures, or posture).

Physiology and Emotion

Reactions to threats are innate, caused by arousal of the autonomic nervous system (ANS).

Sympathetic

The sympathetic branch of the ANS activates the body for emergency action–that is, flight or fight.

Lie Detectors

Lie detectors detect *physiological arousal* caused by lying. Results are not always accurate.

Parasympathetic

The parasympathetic branch of the ANS reverses emotional arousal.

Sudden Death

An overreaction to intense emotion is called a *parasympathetic rebound*. If it is too severe, it can cause death.

Suppressing Emotions

Emotions may be suppressed when necessary.

Primary Emotions

Eight primary emotions (*fear, surprise, sadness, disgust, anger, anticipation, joy, and trust*) have been identified.

Moods

Low-intensity emotional states can last for many hours, or even days.

Brain and Emotion

With the way the brain processes emotions, it is possible to have two emotions at the same time.

Right Hemisphere

Negative emotions are processed here.

Left Hemisphere

Positive emotions are processed here.

Emotional Expression and Theories of Emotion

Next to our own feelings, the expressions of others are the most familiar aspect of emotion.

Emotional Expression

Psychologists believe that emotional expressions evolved to communicate our feelings to others, which aided in survival.

Facial Expressions

The facial expressions of *fear, anger, disgust, sadness*, and *happiness* are recognized around the world.

Body Language

Much communication takes place through facial and bodily expressions of emotion.

Gender and Emotion

Private experiences of emotion appear not to be gender based.

Culture and Emotion

Culture may influence behavioral expressions of emotion.

Theories of Emotion

Theories of emotion vary. Each may offer a part of the truth.

James-Lange

Emotional feelings follow bodily arousal in this theory.

Cannon-Bard

Emotional feelings and arousal occur at the same time here.

Schachter

Mental factors enter into emotion. Interpretation of the arousal (including facial expression) determines the emotion we experience.

Contemporary Model

In modern theory, an *appraisal* is made of an emotional stimulus causing ANS arousal and innate emotional expressions. At the same time, adaptive behaviors are enacted.

1. _____ refers to the ways in which our actions are initiated, sustained, directed, and terminated.
   a. Need
   b. Emotion
   c. Motivation
   d. Learning

2. A goal's appeal beyond its ability to fulfill the need is known as
   a. additional value.
   b. stimulus value.
   c. motivational value.
   d. incentive value.

3. Which of the following is the correct sequence of the model of motivation?
   a. drive-need-response-goal attainment
   b. need-drive-response-goal attainment
   c. need-drive-goal attainment-response
   d. drive-need-goal attainment-response

4. The psychological expression known as "hunger" corresponds to which aspect of motivation?
   a. need
   b. drive
   c. goal
   d. goal attainment

5. _____ motives, such as curiosity and exploration, express our needs for stimulation and information.
   a. Stimulus
   b. Secondary
   c. Primary
   d. None of the above.

6. The body's optimal level of functioning, or its "steady state," is known as
   a. equilibrium incentives.
   b. circadian rhythms.
   c. homeostasis.
   d. learning.

7. After eating a hotdog while watching a baseball game, Caleb became nauseous. Caleb no longer likes hotdogs. This is an example of a(n)
   a. operant conditioning.
   b. taste aversion.
   c. prototype.
   d. yo-yo dieting.

8. Which of the following would not be recommended as a means of behavioral dieting?
   a. exercising
   b. counting calories
   c. keeping a "diet diary"
   d. strengthening your eating cues

9. Which of the following is the eating disorder characterized by extremely low weight?
   a. obesity
   b. anorexia
   c. bulimia
   d. None of the above.

10. Thirst that results from bleeding or sweating is known as _____ thirst.
    a. extracellular
    b. intracellular
    c. intercellular
    d. primary

11. Which of the following describes the inverted U hypothesis?
    a. You will not perform well at very low levels of arousal.
    b. You will not perform well at very high levels of arousal.
    c. There is an optimum level of arousal for peak performance.
    d. All of the above.

12. Which of the following are true according to the arousal theory?
    a. There are ideal levels of activation for various activities.
    b. People become uncomfortable when arousal is too low or too high.

c. Most adults vary their activities to keep arousal at moderate levels.
    d. All of these are true.

13. The Yerkes-Dodson law states that
    a. if a task is complex, arousal should be high.
    b. if a task is simple, arousal should low.
    c. if a task is complex, arousal should low.
    d. there is no relationship between task complexity and appropriate arousal levels.

14. In order for Josh to avoid test anxiety, he may be encouraged to do all of the following except
    a. increase preparation.
    b. learn self-relaxation skills.
    c. rehearse coping skills.
    d. ignore any troubling or disturbing thoughts.

15. _____ is a desire to meet an internal standard of excellence.
    a. Need for achievement
    b. Need for success
    c. Craving for accomplishment
    d. Need for power

16. Which of the following is the correct order of Maslow's hierarchy of needs, from the bottom of the pyramid to the top of the pyramid?
    a. physiological, safety, esteem, love and belonging, self-actualization
    b. self-actualization, esteem, safety, love and belonging, physiological
    c. physiological, safety, love and belonging, esteem, self-actualization
    d. physiological, esteem, love and belonging, safety, self-actualization

17. If Laurie bakes cakes simply because she enjoys it, we would say this activity is one of _____ motivation.
    a. secondary
    b. primary
    c. intrinsic
    d. extrinsic

18. Which of the following characterizes emotion?
    a. subjective feelings
    b. changes in facial expressions
    c. physiological arousal
    d. All of the above.

19. According to the _____ theory, emotional feelings and bodily arousal occur at the same time.
    a. Cannon-Bard
    b. James-Lang
    c. Schachter's cognitive
    d. Spencer-Sweet

20. Which of the following is not considered an element of emotional intelligence?
    a. self-awareness
    b. apathy
    c. managing emotions
    d. emotional flexibility

MODULE 10.1

Overview of Personality

Personality refers to the consistency in who you are, have been, and will become.

Personality

Personality refers to a person's unique pattern of thinking, behaving, and expressing feelings.

Personality

Personality is the special blend of talents, values, hopes, loves, hates, and habits that make us each unique.

Personality Types

A *personality type* refers to people who have several traits in common (e.g., introverts vs. extroverts).

Personality Traits

Traits are stable qualities a person shows in most situations.
1. Traits are inferred from behavior.
2. Once identified, they can be used to predict future behavior.
3. Trait consistencies can span many years.

Personality Theories

Personality theories are systems of concepts, assumptions, ideas, and principles used to explain personality.

Trait Theories

Trait theories attempt to discover what traits make up personality.

Psychodynamic Theories

These theories focus on inner working of personality, especially internal conflicts.

Behavioral and Social Learning Theories

These theories place importance on the external environment and the effects of conditioning and learning.

Humanistic Theories

Humanistic theories stress private, subjective experience, and personal growth.

Personality Is Not

Character

Character and personality are not the same. *Character* implies an evaluation of personality.

Temperament

Temperament refers to the "raw material" from which personalities are formed—that is, the hereditary aspects of personality.

Self-Concept

Self-concept consists of your ideas, perceptions, and feelings about yourself. It includes your sense of self-esteem.

Permanently "Wired In"

Personality slowly matures during old age as people become more conscientious and agreeable.

MODULE 10.2

Trait Theories

The dominant approach to the study of personality is the trait approach. Trait theories attempt to analyze, classify, and interrelate traits.

Common Traits

Characteristics shared by most members of a culture (e.g., Competitiveness is a fairly common trait in America).

Central and Cardinal Traits

Central traits are basic building blocks of personality. *Cardinal traits* are so basic that all their activities can be traced back to the trait.

Source Traits

Source traits are the deeper characteristics or dimensions of the personality.

Individual Traits

Describe a person's unique qualities (e.g., Your American friend is low in competitiveness).

Secondary Traits

Secondary traits are more superficial qualities such as preferences, opinions, and tastes that may change.

Surface Traits

Surface traits are the more visible features of the personality.

The Big-Five Factors

1. *Extroversion:* Level of extroversion vs. introversion.
2. *Agreeableness:* How friendly, nurturing, and caring a person is.
3. *Conscientious:* Level of self-discipline, responsibility, and achievement orientation.
4. *Neuroticism:* How anxious, irritable, and unhappy a person is.
5. *Openness to experience:* How intelligent and open to new ideas a person is.

Psychoanalytic Theory

Freud evolved a theory of personality that discussed the structure of personality, levels of awareness, and the stages of personality development.

Structure of Personality

Freud's model portrays personality as a dynamic system directed by three mental structures.

Id
The id operates on the pleasure principle and is made up of innate biological instincts and urges.

Ego
The ego directs the id's energies and focuses on the reality principle.

Superego
The superego acts as a judge or censor for the thoughts and actions of the ego.

Levels of Awareness

Personal awareness operates on three levels: the conscious, preconscious, and unconscious.

Conscious
The id operates on the pleasure principle and is made up of innate biological instincts and urges.

Preconscious
The id operates on the pleasure principle and is made up of innate biological instincts and urges.

Unconscious
The unconscious holds repressed memories and emotions, plus the instinctual drives of the id.

Personality Development

Personality development occurs in four psychosexual stages: *oral, anal, phallic,* and *genital.*

Freud's Psychosexual Stages

Oral Stage
During the first year of life, most pleasure comes from stimulation of the mouth.

Anal Stage
Between ages 1 and 3, a child can gain approval or express rebellion/aggression by "holding on" or "letting go" during toilet training.

Phallic Stage
Phallic fixations develop between ages 3 and 6. Adult traits of phallic personality are vanity, exhibitionism, sensitive pride, and narcissism.

Genital Stage
The genital stage begins at puberty; it is marked by an upswing in sexual energies; and ends with a mature capacity for love and the realization of full adult sexuality.

Notes

_____

_____

_____

_____

_____

_____

_____

MODULE 10.4

Behavioral and Social Learning Theories

Behavioral and social learning theories are based on scientific research (unlike psychodynamic theories).

Behavioral

Learning theories emphasize that personality is a collection of learned behavior patterns.

View of Personality Development

Personality is acquired through:
- Classical and operant conditioning
- Observational learning
- Reinforcement
- Extinction
- Generalization and discrimination

Personality Structure

Habits make up the structure of personality. Habits are governed by:
- Drives
- Responses
- Cues
- Rewards

Social Learning

Social learning theory is often called *cognitive behaviorism*. It focuses on the social situation, expectancy, and reinforcement value to explain personality.

View of Personality Development

Personality is acquired through:
- Learning principles
- Modeling
- Thought patterns
- Perceptions and expectations
- Beliefs and goals
- Emotions and social relationships

Psychological Situation

How we interpret or define a situation.

Expectancy

Whether or not our response will be reinforced may determine how we act.

Reinforcement Value

Different reinforcements have different values.

MODULE 10.5

Humanistic Theories

Humanistic theories pay special attention to the fuller use of human potentials. Humanism focuses on human experience, problems, potentials, and ideals. It emphasizes an inherently good view of human nature, freedom of choice, and subjective experiences.

Abraham Maslow

Maslow's theory of *self-actualization* emphasized people who were living rich, creative, and satisfying lives.

Self-Actualization

Self-actualization is the process of fully developing personal potentials. It is characterized by a continuous search for personal fulfillment.

Characteristics of Self-Actualizers

Self-actualizers feel safe, nonanxious, accepted, loved, loving, and alive.

Carl Rogers' Theory

Carl Rogers emphasized the *self*.

Self-Image

Attempts to maintain *congruence* between our *self-image* and our *actions* explain many behaviors.

View of Development

Children develop conditions of *worth*, positive *self-regard*, and *organismic valuing* when they are given unconditional positive regard from others.

Positive Psychology

Positive psychologists have identified six human strengths contributing to well-being: wisdom and knowledge, courage, humanity, justice, temperance, transcendence.

Personality Assessment

Measuring personality can help predict how people will behave at work, school, and therapy. Psychologists use a variety of methods to measure personality.

Interviews

Interviews may be either:
1. *Unstructured* (with topics discussed as they arise)
2. *Structured* (with a planned series of questions).

Advantages and Limitations

An interview allows tone of *voice* and *body language* to be observed. However, *preconceptions* or *deceit* may influence the interviewer.

Direct Observation

Direct observation may provide information about personality.

Rating Scales

Rating scales (lists of personality traits or behaviors) can be used to overcome observer misperceptions.

Situational Testing

Simulated real-life situations allow for observation of reactions (such as frustration, anger, or boredom).

Personality Questionnaires

Questionnaires are more objective than interviews or observation.

Projective Tests

Projective tests use ambiguous stimuli to uncover hidden or unconscious wishes, thoughts, and needs.

Rorshach Inkblot Test

The Rorshach test, one of the best-known projective tests, uses descriptions of standard inkblots to detect emotional disturbances.

Limitations of Projective Testing

Projective tests are considered to be the least valid tests of personality because the scorer has to interpret the responses.

Notes

---

1. _____ refers to a person's unique pattern of thinking, emotions, and behavior.
   a. Temperament
   c. Character
   b. Personality
   d. Charisma

2. You are told by a friend that they want you to meet someone they know who is nice, honest, outgoing, and friendly. As described in the text, they are most accurately describing to you the person's
   a. character.
   c. inherent value.
   b. personality.
   d. temperament.

3. A personality _____ refers to people who have several traits in common.
   a. illness
   c. combination
   b. trait
   d. type

4. Which people might describe themselves as stupid, worthless, or a failure?
   a. People with high self-esteem.
   b. People with moderate self-esteem.
   c. People with low self-esteem.
   d. All of these people.

5. Your psychology instructor asks you to write a paper that answers the question, "Who am I?" The most likely title for this paper would be
   a. My Self-Concept.
   c. My Self-Esteem.
   b. Personality and Me.
   d. none of the above.

6. _____ theories focus on the inner workings of personality, especially internal conflicts and struggles.
   a. Cognitive
   c. Psychodynamic
   b. Behavioral
   d. Trait

7. Which of the following is not one of the Big Five personality factors identified in the text?
   a. Curiosity
   c. Extroversion
   b. Agreeableness
   d. Neuroticism

8. Traits shared by most members of a culture are referred to as _____ traits.
   a. type
   c. individualistic
   b. cardinal
   d. common

9. According to Freud, which part of the personality acts as the negotiator or decision maker?
   a. Id
   c. Superego
   b. Ego
   d. Conscious self

10. According to the text, the _____ mind contains material that can be easily brought to awareness.
    a. conscious
    c. subconscious
    b. unconscious
    d. preconscious

11. Identify the correct order of Freud's psychosexual stages.
    a. Anal, oral, phallic, genital
    b. Oral, anal, genital, phallic
    c. Oral, anal, phallic, genital
    d. Phallic, anal, oral, genital

12. _____ theories emphasize that personality is acquired through classical and operant conditioning, observational learning, reinforcement, extinction, generalization, and discrimination.
    a. Psychodynamic
    c. Behavioral
    b. Trait
    d. Humanistic

13. Habits are governed by all of the following elements of learning, except
    a. goal.
    b. drive.
    c. cue.
    d. response.

14. What did Albert Bandura call the capacity for producing a desired result?
    a. Self-esteem
    b. Self-efficacy
    c. Self-reinforcement
    d. Self-concept

15. Which of the following is not one of Dollard and Miller's four critical situations?
    a. Feeding
    b. Sex training
    c. Social inclusion
    d. Toilet training

16. Jacob states that someday he hopes to be just like his dad: funny, brave, tough, and caring. This might be referred to as Jacob's _____.
    a. self-actualization
    b. perfect self
    c. ideal self
    d. potential personality

17. Chris tells his daughters that he will always accept them and love them, regardless of what they do or don't do. Chris's daughters have received what Rogers would refer to as
    a. authoritative parenting.
    b. unconditional positive regard.
    c. self-actualization.
    d. unrestricted valuing.

18. In which of the following is information regarding one's personality gathered by asking a planned series of questions?
    a. Structured interview
    b. Unstructured interview
    c. Situational test
    d. All of the above

19. One of the best-known and most widely used objective personality tests is the
    a. Guilford-Zimmerman Temperament Survey.
    b. 16 PF.
    c. MMPI - 2.
    d. California Psychological Inventory.

20. The Rorschach Inkblot Test is an example of a(n) _____ personality test.
    a. projective
    b. objective
    c. subjective
    d. predictive

Health Psychology

Health psychology aims to use behavioral principles to prevent illness and promote health.

- Health-promoting behaviors: Some diseases can be treated or prevented by making relatively minor but very specific changes in behavior.

- Community health: Community programs that educate larger numbers of people often offer services such as screenings, advice, and even treatment.

- Early prevention: Often, learning how to not start a risky behavior can do much to prevent the development of a disease.

Stress, Frustration, and Conflict

Although a natural part of life, stress can be a major behavioral risk factor if it is prolonged or severe. Stress is the mental and physical condition that occurs when we adapt to the environment.

Appraising Stressors

Ultimately, stress depends on how we perceive a situation. Do we view it as a *thrill or a threat*?

Conflict

Conflict occurs when contradictory choices must be made.

Frustration

Frustration occurs when obstacles prevent us from reaching desired goals.

Primary and Secondary Appraisal

We need to assess the situation:
1. *Primary Appraisal*
   Is the situation relevant to us?
2. *Secondary Appraisal*
   What can we do about it if it is?

When Is Stress a Pain?

Stressors (events that challenge or threaten) may be unpredictable or there may be a time limit (*pressure*).
This is known as distress.

Types of Conflict

The five major types of conflict are:
- *Approach-approach*
- *Avoidance-avoidance*
- *Approach-avoidance*
- *Double approach-avoidance*
- *Multiple approach-avoidance*

Obstacles

External frustrations are represented by conditions outside the individual. *Personal frustrations* stem from personal characteristics.

Coping with Threat

If we appraise a situation as a threat, we can use:
1. *Problem*-focused coping
   or
2. *Emotion*-focused coping

Stress Elements

Intense, repeated, or *uncontrolled* stressors related to pressure will magnify stress.

Coping with Conflict

1. Don't be hasty when making important decisions.
2. Try out important decisions partially when possible.
3. Look for workable compromises.
4. When all else fails, make a decision and live with it.

Reactions to Frustration

Reactions to frustration include *persistence, more vigorous responding, circumvention, direct aggression, displaced aggression,* and *escape/withdrawal.*

Coping with Frustration

1. Identify the source of frustration.
2. Is the source something that can be changed?
3. If the source can be changed or removed, are the efforts worth it?
Distinguish between *real* barriers and *imagined* barriers.

Defenses, Helplessness, and Depression

We react to threatening experiences and anxiety in various ways.

Psychological Defense Mechanisms

A psychological defense mechanism is any mental process used to avoid, deny, or distort sources of threat or anxiety, especially threats to one's self-image.

Denial
Protecting oneself from an unpleasant reality by refusing to accept it or believe it.

Repression
Protecting oneself by repressing threatening thoughts and impulses.

Reaction Formation
Repressing impulses by exaggerating opposite behavior.

Regression
Any return to earlier, less demanding situations or habits.

Projection
An unconscious process that protects us from the anxiety we would feel if we were to discern our faults.

Rationalization
Justifying personal actions by giving "rational" but false reasons for them.

Compensation
Going to unusual lengths to overcome a weakness or excel in other areas.

Sublimation
Working off frustrated desires through socially acceptable activities.

Learned Helplessness

Learned helplessness is an acquired inability to overcome obstacles and avoid aversive stimuli. Occurs when events appear to be *uncontrollable*.

Hope
Hope and a feeling of control are essential to overcoming learned helplessness or depression.

Depression

Depression is a widespread emotional problem. Learned helplessness and depression share many similarities.

Recognizing Depression
Depression is marked by feelings of despondency, powerlessness, and overwhelming hopelessness.

Notes

Stress and Health

Psychologists have established that stress has many effects on our health by reducing the body's natural defenses against disease.

Life Events and Stress
Life events, both major and minor, can impact our health in a many ways.

Social Readjustment Rating Scale (SRRS)
Life changes (good and bad) can increase risk of accidents or illness. Life change units (LCUs) from the SRRS rank the importance of events to the changes in health 1 or 2 years later.

Hazzards and Hassles
Frequent, severe *hassles (microstressors)* predict day-to-day health.

Psychosomatic Disorders
Psychosomatic disorders are real disorders where psychological factors contribute to bodily damage.

NOT Hypochondriasis!
People suffering from psychosomatic disorders face asthma, migraine headaches, or high blood pressure, NOT imagined diseases.

Most Common Problems
Gastrointestinal and respiratory problems are the most frequently reported psychosomatic problems.

Personality Types
Personality, genetic differences, organ weakness, and learned reactions to stress can all enter into the stress picture.

Cardiac Personality
Among other characteristics, Type A personalities are *chronically angry* and are also at risk for heart attacks.

Hardy Personality
The hardy personality shares many of the same characteristics as the Type A but does not become ill as often.

Stress, Illness, and the Immune System
Prolonged stress can weaken the immune system, thus creating opportunity for serious health risks.

Psychoneuroimmunology
This specialty studies the links among behavior, stress, disease, and the immune system.

Boosting Immune System
Various psychological approaches, such as support groups, relaxation exercises, guided imagery, and stress management training, can boost immune system functioning.

Stress Management

Stress management is the use of behavioral strategies to reduce stress and improve coping skills.

Ways to Manage Bodily Reactions to Stress

Exercise
Any full-body exercise can be effective for managing stress. Choose vigorous yet enjoyable activities and do them daily!

Meditation
Meditation is often recommended for quieting the body and promoting relaxation. Meditation is one of the most effective ways to relax.

Progressive Relaxation
By tightening all the muscles in a given area of your body, then voluntarily relaxing them, you are engaging in progressive relaxation.

Guided Imagery
In guided imagery, you visualize images that are calming, relaxing, or beneficial in other ways.

Ways to Minimize Ineffective Behavior When You Are Stressed Out

Slow Down
Stress can be self-generated, so try to do things at a slower pace.

Get Organized
Disorganization causes stress . . . so get organized! Set priorities and keep it simple (KIS).

Balance Work and Relaxation
Damaging stress often comes from letting one element, such as work or school, get blown out of proportion.

Accept Your Limits
Set gradual, achievable goals and realistic limits on what you try to do on any given day. Learn to say: NO!

Write About Your Feelings
Several studies have found that writing about your thoughts and feelings allows you to better cope with stress, experience fewer illnesses, and get better grades!

Notes

_____

_____

_____

_____

_____

_____

_____

1. Health psychology uses behavioral principles to prevent _____ and promote _____.
   a. problems, communication
   b. illness, health
   c. mental illness, psychotropic medications
   d. All of the above.

2. Strokes and lung cancer are just two examples of _____ diseases.
   a. lifestyle
   b. personality
   c. behavioral medicine
   d. contagious

3. _____ are actions that increase the chances of disease, injury, or early death.
   a. Cognitive variables
   b. Health-complicating events
   c. Combination health threats
   d. Behavioral risk factors

4. Mitch is an anxious and irritable individual who has poor eating and sleeping habits, which leave him frequently ill. Mitch might be described as having a _____ personality.
   a. health-compromised
   b. hardy
   c. resilient
   d. disease-prone

5. The "Just Say No" campaign for preventing drug use would be considered a _____.
   a. refusal skills training program
   b. psychodynamic training program
   c. life skills training program
   d. resistance prevention program

6. _____ is the mental and physical condition that occurs when we adjust or adapt to the environment.
   a. Anxiety
   b. Stress
   c. Trauma
   d. Apprehension

7. If a person is under prolonged stress for an extended period, he or she may experience the
   a. general adaptation syndrome.
   b. rejuvenation effect.
   c. autonomic rebound.
   d. anxiety response disorder.

8. If Brad decided that after graduation, he wanted to find a job studying the links among behavior, stress, disease, and the immune system, he would probably be looking into the field of
   a. medical psychology.
   b. neuropsychology.
   c. eating disorders.
   d. psychoneuroimmunology.

9. Stress is typically considered more damaging when it is
   a. unpredictable yet controllable.
   b. predictable but not controllable.
   c. predictable and controllable.
   d. neither predictable nor controllable.

10. A(n) _____ appraisal is one in which you decide if a situation is relevant or irrelevant, positive or threatening.
    a. initial
    b. secondary
    c. essential
    d. primary

11. When she heard the bad news, Emily concentrated on not crying in front of her children. This might be considered what kind of coping?
    a. Behavior focused
    b. Solution focused
    c. Problem focused
    d. Emotion focused

12. When Connor got caught in traffic on his way to take his final exam, he experienced an _____ frustration.
    a. academic
    b. inherent
    c. internal
    d. external

13. Reactions to frustration include all of the following except
    a. less vigorous responding.
    b. persistence.
    c. scapegoating.
    d. displaced aggression.

14. Having to choose between writing your term paper or going to your friend's birthday party would be described by the text as an example of
    a. anxiety.
    b. stress.
    c. frustration.
    d. conflict.

15. In the _____ conflict, one must choose between two pleasant or desirable options.
    a. avoidance-avoidance
    b. approach-avoidance
    c. approach-approach
    d. double approach-avoidance

16. Ty stated, in defense of his getting caught shoplifting, that the store had probably overcharged him on numerous occasions and therefore owed him the items taken. This would be an example of which defense mechanism?
    a. Rationalization
    b. Denial
    c. Projection
    d. Regression

17. _____ is an acquired inability to overcome obstacles and avoid aversive stimuli.
    a. Learned hopelessness
    b. Learned helplessness
    c. Educated-actualization
    d. Dysfunctional cognition

18. What do you call someone who believes he has a serious disease or illness even though there is no medical evidence of its presence?
    a. College student during finals week
    b. Malingerer
    c. Hypochondriac
    d. All of the above

19. Friedman and Rosenman (1983) classified people who have a _____ risk of cardiac problems as Type A personalities.
    a. low
    b. medium
    c. high
    d. no

20. Which of the following is not one of the three goals for reducing hostility as described by the text?
    a. Learn to be kinder.
    b. Reduce feelings of anger.
    c. Stop mistrusting the motives of others.
    d. Learn to use humor more readily.

Chapter 12

Psychological Disorders

Normality and Psychopathology

Determining if a person's behavior is abnormal can be difficult.

Classifying Mental Disorders

A *mental disorder* is a serious impairment in psychological functioning. The *Diagnostic and Statistical Manual of Mental Disorders* (DSM-IV-TR, 2000) helps correctly identify mental disorders.

Normality—What Is Normal?

The term *psychopathology* refers to both the scientific study of mental, emotional, and behavioral disorders and also the disorders themselves.

Abnormality

It is possible to vary from the norm in a variety of ways. Depending on the context in which the variation occurs, it may be seen as psychopathology.

Major Mental Disorders

Major mental problems include *psychotic, organic, mood, anxiety, somatoform, dissociative, personality, sexual or gender identity*, and *substance-related* disorders.

Subjective Discomfort

A sense of *subjective discomfort* (private feelings of pain, unhappiness, or emotional distress) or a lack of discomfort when it would be appropriate may be a sign of psychopathology.

Disordered Behavior

Two core features are key to abnormality:
- The behavior is *maladaptive* (prevents day-to-day normal coping).
- There is a *loss of control* over the behavior.

Social Noncomformity

Social nonconformity may be a sign of mental disorder. However, the context of the nonconformity is important.

Statistical Abnormality

Statistical abnormality refers to scoring very high or low on some dimension, such as intelligence, anxiety, or depression.

Insanity

Insanity is a legal term referring to an inability to manage one's affairs or see the consequences of one's actions.

Notes

_____

_____

_____

_____

_____

_____

_____

Personality and Anxiety-Based Disorders

Personality and anxiety disorders can make life very difficult and be very debilitating.

Personality Disorders

Maladaptive personality patterns are referred to as *personality disorders*.

Antisocial Personality

An antisocial personality is one (*sometimes called a sociopath*) who lacks a conscience, is impulsive, selfish, dishonest, emotionally shallow, and manipulative.

Sociopaths . . . Dangerous?

Sociopaths or psychopaths are poorly socialized and seem to be incapable of feeling guilt, shame, fear, loyalty, or love. Many are delinquents or criminals who may be a threat to the public.

Common Behaviors

Sociopaths have been found to be "blind" to the signs of disgust in others. This may add to their capacity for cruelty and their ability to coldly use others and cheat their way through life.

Causes

People with antisocial personalities were typically emotionally deprived, neglected, and abused as children.

Stress and Dissociative Disorders

Stress disorders occur when people experience stresses outside the range of normal human experience. Dissociative disorders show amnesia, fugue, or multiple identities.

Acute Stress Disorder

Acute stress disorder occurs when traumatic events (combat, rape, etc.) lead to reactions that last LESS than a month after the event.

Posttraumatic Stress Disorder

Posttraumatic stress disorder occurs when violent, traumatic events (combat, rape, etc.) lead to reactions that last MORE than a month. Symptoms include insomnia, nightmares, wariness, and reliving of the traumatic event.

Dissociative Disorders

Dissociations are often triggered by highly traumatic events the individual wishes to flee. Dissociative disorders may take the form of amnesia, fugue, and dissociative identity disorder (commonly known as multiple personalities).

Causes

Traumatic events, such as floods, earthquakes, and horrible accidents, can lead to the stress disorders. Highly traumatic events, such as prolonged and extreme abuse, are common to the dissociative disorders.

Anxiety-Based Disorders

Anxiety refers to feelings of apprehension, dread, or uneasiness. In anxiety disorders, these feelings are extreme, out of control, and self-defeating.

Panic Disorder

Panic disorder causes people to feel sudden, intense, unexpected panic (may occur with or without agoraphobia–fear of embarrassment in unfamiliar situations).

Phobias

Phobias involve fear and avoidance of particular objects, activities, or situations.

Obsessive-Compulsive Disorder

Obsessive-compulsive disorder involves preoccupation with distressing thoughts and a need to perform certain behaviors.

Somatoform Disorders

Somatoform disorders center on physical complaints that mimic disease or disability.

Causes

In most anxiety disorders, distress seems greatly out of proportion to a person's circumstances. It may also underlie the dissociative and somatoform disorders, where maladaptive behavior serves to reduce anxiety and discomfort.

Psychosis, Delusional Disorders, and Schizophrenia

Psychotic disorders are among the most serious of all mental problems.

Psychosis

Psychosis is a loss of contact with reality. Hallucinations and delusions, disturbed thought and emotions, and personality disorganization are common.

Delusions

False beliefs (against all contrary evidence) about yourself or others are *delusions*.

Hallucinations

When you have imaginary sensations (seeing, smelling, tasting, or hearing things that are not there) you are having *hallucinations*.

Organic Psychosis

Psychosis may occur because of brain injury or disease (old age, stroke, Alzheimer's disease, etc.).

Paranoid Psychosis

Paranoid psychosis is a common delusional disorder. Treatment is rare because the individual resists treatment as part of the "conspiracy."

Delusional Disorders

People with delusional disorders have an unmistakable break with reality that may involve paranoia, jealousy, delusions of grandeur, or personal capabilities. The main feature of the delusional disorders is the presence of deeply held false beliefs.

Erotomanic Type

Erotomanic types have erotic delusions that they are loved by another person, especially by someone famous or of higher status.

Grandiose Type

People with this disorder suffer from the delusion that they have some great, unrecognized talent, knowledge, or insight.

Jealous Type

People with this type of delusion have an all-consuming, but unfounded, belief that their spouse or lover is unfaithful.

Persecutory Type

Persecutory types have delusions of persecution, such as being conspired against, cheated on, spied on, followed, poisoned, maligned, or harassed.

Somatic Type

People with somatic type delusions believe that their body is diseased, rotting, or infested with insects or parasites, or that parts of their body are defective.

Schizophrenia

The most common form of psychosis is schizophrenia. Delusions, hallucinations, inappropriate emotions, and thinking abnormalities are all found in schizophrenia.

Major Subtypes

Schizophrenics may develop one of four subtypes:
- *Disorganized*
- *Catatonic*
- *Paranoid*
- *Undifferentiated*

Causes of Schizophrenia

Possible causes of schizophrenia include *environment* (including teratogens), *heredity*, and *brain chemistry*.

Notes

Mood Disorders

Mood disorders, major disturbances in emotion, are the most common disorders of all. Brain chemistry, learned behaviors, stress, genetics, and culture have been cited as possible causes of mood disorders.

Depressive Disorder

Exaggerated, prolonged, or unreasonable sadness and despondency are signs of *depressive disorders.*

Major Depressive Disorder

When the person suffers a steep emotional depression.

Dysthymic Disorder

When the person suffers a mild depression for at least 2 years.

Bipolar Disorders

Exaggerated, prolonged, or unreasonable sadness and despondency that alternate with manic episodes of varying degree, are signs of the bipolar disorders.

Bipolar I Disorder

People who experience both extreme mania and deep depression suffer from *bipolar I disorder.*

Bipolar II Disorder

In *bipolar II* disorder the person is mostly sad and guilt ridden but has had at least one mildly manic episode.

Notes

_____

_____

_____

_____

_____

_____

Psychology in Action: Suicide—Lives on the Brink

Why do people commit suicide?

Mental Disorders

A diagnosable mental disorder, such as depression or substance abuse, is a factor in 90 percent of all suicides.

Substance Abuse

Drug and alcohol abuse impairs judgment and moods.

Anger and Aggression

Antisocial, impulsive, or aggressive behaviors are major risk factors for suicide.

Prior Suicide Attempts

A previous attempt, or family history of suicidal behavior are risk factors.

Feelings of Social Rejection

Shame, humiliation, failure and isolation are all risk factors.

Availability of a Firearm

Combined with other risk factors, simply having access to a firearm can be lethal.

Feelings of Hopelessness

When combined with an extremely negative self-image, feelings of hopelessness can indicate a very HIGH risk of suicide.

1. _____ refers to the scientific study of mental, emotional, and behavioral disorders.
   a. Abnormal psychology
   b. Psychopathology
   c. Psychopathy
   d. Behaviorism

2. Upon what criteria might someone with red hair be considered abnormal?
   a. Personal distress
   b. Social nonconformity
   c. Statistical abnormality
   d. Interference with daily functioning

3. In the United States, psychological problems are classified using what manual?
   a. DSM-IV-TR
   b. ICM-10
   c. 16 PF
   d. No manual is necessary; only clinical opinion is required.

4. A person with a significant impairment in psychological functioning might be diagnosed with a
   a. psychological disease.
   b. brain illness.
   c. mental disorder.
   d. psychotic issue.

5. Due to his drug use, Chad now has impaired memory, an altered personality, and fluctuating moods. Chad would be diagnosed with a(n)
   a. organic mental disorder.
   b. impaired brain disease.
   c. mood disorder.
   d. stress-related illness.

6. _____ is a word that has been replaced by the term *anxiety*.
   a. Neurosis
   b. Stress
   c. Trauma
   d. Nervous

7. Tara's sexual identity does not match her gender and therefore results in personal discomfort. Tara may be diagnosed with a
   a. paraphilia.
   b. sexual confusion disorder.
   c. gender-identity disorder.
   d. mood disorder.

8. Temporary psychological amnesia, fugue and multiple personality are classified as _____ disorders.
   a. dissociative
   b. anxiety
   c. psychotic
   d. somatoform

9. Which of the following factors contribute to psychopathology?
   a. Family factors
   b. Social factors
   c. Psychological factors
   d. All of the above can contribute to psychopathology.

10. Being *insane* refers to
    a. any psychiatric diagnosis.
    b. a legal declaration indicating an inability to manage one's own affairs or foresee the consequences of their actions.
    c. the psychiatric diagnosis indicating that an individual is suffering from a severe and persistent mental illness.
    d. a requirement for involuntary hospitalization.

11. A person who has trouble forming close relationships because he is emotionally shallow, dishonest, and manipulative may be diagnosed with
    a. major depression.
    b. acute stress.
    c. antisocial personality disorder.
    d. mental retardation.

12. If Glenda suffers from chronic anxiety and stays in her home because she is afraid of having another panic attack in public, a psychologist might consider her to have the diagnosis of
    a. panic attack with agoraphobia.
    b. acute anxiety.
    c. social phobia.
    d. adjustment disorder.

13. A _____ is an intense, irrational fear.
    a. stimulus
    b. phobia
    c. obsession
    d. generalized anxiety

14. In obsessive-compulsive disorder, the obsession is the _____, whereas the compulsion is the _____.
    a. thought; behavior
    b. control; thought
    c. consequence; antecedent
    d. stimulus; control

15. A person who suffers from more than one disorder at a time would be considered to have _____ illnesses.
    a. stress-related
    b. dissociative
    c. recurrent
    d. comorbid

16. In a somatoform illness (such as conversion disorder), people convert _____ conflicts into ones that resemble _____ _____ problems.
    a. group; personal
    b. physical; medical
    c. emotional; physical
    d. psychological; emotional

17. The term _____ refers to internal motives, conflicts, unconscious forces, and other dynamics of mental life.
    a. cognitive
    b. psychodynamic
    c. humanistic
    d. organic

18. Which of the following is not one of the subtypes of schizophrenia?
    a. Catatonic
    b. Disorganized
    c. Organic
    d. Undifferentiated

19. If your friend has been mildly depressed for more than 2 years, he may be suffering from which mood disorder?
    a. Dysthymia
    b. Cyclothymia
    c. Major depression
    d. Bipolar disorder

20. Which of the following is not one of the major risk factors for suicide, as listed in the text?
    a. Increased socialization
    b. Alcohol or drug abuse
    c. Severe anxiety
    d. A history of suicide attempts

Psychotherapy and Psychoanalysis

Psychotherapy refers to any psychological technique that can bring about positive changes in personality, behavior, or personal adjustment.

Psychotherapy

Origins of Therapy
History includes many examples of attempts to deal with mental problems. Humane treatment of the mentally ill began in Paris in 1793.

Primitive Methods
Early treatments for mental problems such as *trepanning* or *demonology* give good reasons to appreciate modern therapies.

Dimensions of Modern Therapy
Therapies may be:

Individual	or	Group
Insight	or	Action oriented
Directive	or	Nondirective
Time limited	or	Open ended
Supportive	or	Positive

Myths
Not all therapies work equally well for all problems. Therapies do not change a person's history.

Freud's Theory of Psychoanalysis
The main goal of psychoanalysis is to reduce internal conflicts that lead to emotional suffering.

Freud's Theory of Psychoanalysis
Freud created the first true psychotherapy 100 years ago. His theory stressed neurosis and hysteria as effects of:
- Repressed memories
- Motives
- Conflicts

Techniques
Freud relied on these techniques:
- Free association
- Dream analysis
- Analysis of resistance
- Analysis of transference

to uncover the unconscious roots of what he termed *neurosis*.

Psychoanalysis Today
The expense and length of treatment have made psychoanalysis a relatively rare treatment today.

Brief Psychodynamic Therapy
A more direct style of therapy uses direct questioning to reveal unconscious conflicts. Modern therapists also provoke emotional reactions that will lower defenses and provide insights.

Notes

_____

_____

_____

_____

_____

_____

_____

Insight Therapies

Insight therapists help clients gain a deeper understanding of their thoughts, emotions, and behavior.

Humanistic Therapies

Humanistic therapies generally assume that it is possible for people to live rich, rewarding lives by using their full potentials.

Psychotherapy at a Distance

Various forms of psychological services are being offered over the phone, Internet, teleconferences, radio, and television. The value of therapy offered by telephone counselors and Internet therapists remains questionable. The best advice being offered is to discuss the problem with a psychologist or counselor in one's own community.

Client-Centered Therapy

Client-centered therapy is *nondirective*, allowing the patient to direct the therapy session. The intent is to gain *insight* while discussing conscious thoughts and feelings.

Goals

Client-centered therapy seeks to uncover a "true self" hidden behind a screen of defenses.

Existential Therapy

Existential therapy is an insight therapy that focuses on the problems of existence, such as meaning, choice, and responsibility. Making choices, and personal responsibility are keystones of this therapy.

Goals

Existential therapy emphasizes free will, the human ability to make choices, and that you can *choose to become* the person you want to be.

Gestalt Therapy

Gestalt therapy is directive and based on the idea that perception is disjointed and incomplete in maladjusted persons. Integration of fragmented experiences into a whole (a Gestalt) is the focus.

Goals

Gestalt therapy helps people rebuild thinking, feeling, and acting into connected wholes.

Behavior Therapy

Behavior therapists use *learning principles* to make constructive changes in behavior patterns. *Behavior modification* refers to any use of classical or operant conditioning to directly alter human behavior.

Healing by Learning

Behavior therapists assume that people have learned their phobias, fears, and anxieties. *Relearning responses* can make changes in a person's quality of life. Aversion therapy and desensitization are based on *classical conditioning*.

Aversion Therapy

In aversion therapy, an individual learns to associate a strong aversion to an undesirable habit.

Desensitization

Desensitization efforts focus on undoing conditioned emotional responses by blocking out the fear.

Performing Aversive Therapy

Aversive therapy can be accomplished by pairing the undesirable habit, such as smoking or drinking, immediately with a negative stimulus, such as shock or pain.

Performing Desensitization

Desensitization can be accomplished through three steps: construction of a hierarchy, relaxation, and performance of least disturbing items on the list.

Uses for Aversive Therapy

Aversive therapy can be used for undesirable habits such as smoking, drinking, gambling, drug addictions (marijuana, cocaine), and stuttering.

Uses for Desensitization

Desensitization is primarily used to help people unlearn phobias or strong anxieties. Vicarious desensitization uses the power of observational learning. Virtual reality exposure facilitates exposure to feared stimuli without the associated risks.

Operant and Cognitive Therapies

Operant and cognitive therapies take contrasting approaches to human problems.

Operant Therapies

Operant therapies are based on the *consequences of behaviors* (operant conditioning).

Cognitive Therapy

In general, cognitive therapy helps change thinking patterns that lead to troublesome emotions or behaviors.

Operant Principles

Positive Reinforcement
Responses that are followed by reward tend to occur more frequently.

Nonreinforcement
A response that is not followed by a reward will occur less frequently.

Extinction
A response that is not followed by a reward many times will eventually go away.

Punishment
A response that is followed by discomfort or an undesirable effect will be suppressed.

Shaping
Successive approximations of a desired behavior are rewarded.

Therapy Example

Reinforcement and Token Economies
By using tokens (symbolic rewards that can be exchanged for real rewards), a therapist can immediately reward positive behaviors.

Stimulus Control
Control of the stimuli in a situation can lead to a response.

Time Out
The individual is rewarded from a situation in which reinforcement is occurring. This is a variation of nonreinforcement.

Cognitive Principles

Rational-Emotive Behavior Therapy (REBT)
Rational-emotive behavior therapy attempts to do away with irrational beliefs that cause many emotional problems. REBT is very directive.

Core Irrational Beliefs
- I must perform well and be approved of by significant others.
- You must treat me fairly.
- Conditions must be the way I want them to be.

Therapy Example

Cognitive Therapy for Depression
Cognitive therapists attempt to change the maladaptive thoughts, beliefs, and feelings that lead to depression or similar problems.

Beck's Basics
Aaron Beck believes depressed persons see themselves, the world, and the future in negative terms. Beck believes depression is a result of three major distortions in thinking:
- Selective perception
- Overgeneralization
- All-or-nothing thinking

Group Therapy, Therapy Skills, and Medical Therapies

Successful therapy is carried out in other important ways.

Group Therapy
Group therapy is often as effective as individual therapy, and it has some advantages.

Psychodrama
Psychodrama (acting out personal conflicts and feelings in the presence of others) allows a person to gain insights that can be transferred to real-life situations.

Family Therapy
In family therapy, husband, wife, and children must work individually and as a group to resolve the problems of each family member.

Group Awareness Training
Encounter groups and sensitivity training groups are often used to improve employee relationships. The claimed benefits may result from a therapy placebo effect.

Psychotherapy
Some general helping skills can be distilled from the various therapy approaches.

Core Features of Psychotherapy
All therapies have four core elements:
1. A caring relationship between client and therapist (therapeutic alliance).
2. Therapy offers a protected setting for catharsis.
3. All therapies offer some extent of explanation for the client's suffering.
4. Clients have a new perspective about themselves and their situations.

Basic Counseling Skills
- Listen actively.
- Clarify the problem.
- Focus on feelings.
- Avoid giving advice.
- Accept the person's frame of reference.
- Reflect thoughts and feelings.
- Use silence in between responses.
- Ask open-ended questions.
- Maintain confidentiality.

Medical Therapies
Major mental disorders (major depressive disorders, schizophrenia, etc.) are most often treated medically.

Drug Therapies
Drugs have shortened hospital stays and improved the chances that people will recover from major psychological disorders.

Electroshock
Electroconvulsive therapy (ECT) involves administering an electric current to the brain in order to end severe depression and suicidal behavior.

Psychosurgery
Psychosurgery (any surgical alteration of the brain) is a technique with both supporters and detractors.

Psychology in Action: Self-Management and Seeking Professional Help

Self-Management Techniques
Some personal problems can be successfully treated using self-management techniques.

Covert Reinforcement
The use of positive imagery to reinforce desired behavior.

Covert Sensitization
The use of aversive imagery to discourage unwanted behavior.

Thought Stopping
The use of mild punishment to prevent upsetting thoughts.

Self-Directed Desensitization
Pairing relaxation with a hierarchy of upsetting images to lessen fears.

Seeking Professional Help
Seek help if you have psychological discomfort, changes in behavior, suicidal thoughts, or if friends suggest that you may need help. Seek out a mental health association or call a crisis hotline; psychologists are also listed in the phone book. The choice between a psychiatrist and a psychologist can be arbitrary.

1. _____ is any psychological technique used to facilitate positive changes in a person's personality, behavior, or adjustment.
   a. Pharmacotherapy
   b. Directive therapy
   c. Psychotherapy
   d. Positive therapy

2. _____ therapy is any psychotherapy whose goal is to lead clients to a deeper understanding of their thoughts, emotions, and behavior.
   a. Insight
   b. Supportive
   c. Directive
   d. Cognitive

3. _____ created the first recognized psychotherapy.
   a. Albert Bandura
   b. Wilhelm Wundt
   c. Sigmund Freud
   d. Abraham Maslow

4. In dream analysis, the _____ content is to the hidden meaning of the dream.
   a. latent
   b. manifest
   c. indirect
   d. reciprocal

5. _____ is the tendency to assign feelings to a therapist that match those the patient had for important persons in his or her past.
   a. Redesigned assignment
   b. Counter-transference
   c. Transference
   d. Resistance

6. Carl Rogers believed all of the following were essential conditions of therapy, except
   a. empathy.
   b. authenticity.
   c. conditional regard.
   d. reflection.

7. _____ therapy helps people rebuild thinking, feeling, and acting into connected wholes.
   a. Gestalt
   b. Existential
   c. Psychoanalytic
   d. Behavioral

8. The use of classical or operant conditioning to alter behavior is known as _____.
   a. behavioral desensitization
   b. behavior modification
   c. action-oriented therapy
   d. psychoanalysis

9. When an alcoholic takes a medication that results in her getting nauseous following the ingestion of alcohol, she is experiencing a(n) _____ therapy.
   a. physiological
   b. cognitive
   c. aversion
   d. reality

10. By watching his father pet dogs without fear, Carl's fear of dogs gradually began to decrease. This learning is an example of
    a. operant conditioning.
    b. vicarious desensitization.
    c. aversion therapy.
    d. systematic desensitization.

11. Using the therapeutic technique of _____, you might be asked to play the part of someone else in order to increase your understanding of that person.
    a. empathic acting
    b. mirroring
    c. psychodrama
    d. role reversal

12. Which of the following is not considered one of the basic counseling skills discussed in the text?
    a. Accepting the person's frame of reference
    b. Problem clarification
    c. Passive listening
    d. Avoiding giving advice

13. The use of drugs to treat mental illnesses is known as:
    a. pharmacotherapy.
    b. medical therapy.
    c. biopsychotherapy.
    d. psychotherapy.

14. The use of electrical currents to induce seizure activity in the brain to alleviate the symptoms of depression is known as
    a. PET.
    b. psychosurgery.
    c. neuroelectrotherapy.
    d. ECT.

15. _____ is the most extreme medical treatment.
    a. Psychopharmacology
    b. MRI
    c. Psychosurgery
    d. Biofeedback

16. Within a(n) _____ treatment program, patients spend their day at the hospital but go home at night.
    a. inpatient hospitalization
    b. temporary hospitalization
    c. partial hospitalization
    d. sunlight therapy

17. A community mental health (CMH) center is a treatment option typically
    a. serving the upper class or "private pay" clients.
    b. offering a wide range of mental health and psychiatric services.
    c. providing long-term treatment and inpatient care.
    d. utilizing a psychoanalytic approach.

18. Whenever Doug begins to think of himself as a failure, he snaps a rubber band worn around his wrist. This technique is known as
    a. overt desensitization.
    b. covert sensitization.
    c. aversive behaviorism.
    d. thought stopping.

19. _____ offer mutual support and a chance for discussion to members who share a common type of problem.
    a. Paraprofessional groups
    b. Self-help groups
    c. Maintenance groups
    d. Conversation groups

20. Trepanning involves
    a. the use of electric shock in order to induce a convulsion within the patient's brain.
    b. rewarding close approximations of a desired behavior.
    c. the use of psychiatric medications to treat mental illnesses.
    d. boring a hole in a person's head to "release evil spirits" or relieve pressure.

Chapter 14

Sex, Gender, and Androgyny

Sex and gender have a tremendous impact on relationships, personal identity, and health. In sexual development, being male or female is both biological *(sex)* and psychological *(gender)*.

Biological Dimensions of Sex

When classifying a person as male or female, we must take into account many factors:

- Genetic sex (chromosomes)
- Gonadal sex (ovaries or testes)
- Hormonal sex (proportion of androgens or estrogens)
- Genital sex (clitoris, vagina, penis, and scrotum)
- Gender identity (one's subjective sense of maleness or femaleness)

Prenatal Sexual Development

Genetic sex is determined at conception with the combination of XX or XY chromosomes.

Female or Male?

Males differ in both primary (sexual and reproductive organs) and secondary (superficial physical features that appear at puberty) sexual characteristics.

Sex Hormones

Sex differences are related to the proportion of estrogens (female hormones) and androgens (male hormones) found in both male and female bodies.

Psychological Origins of Male-Female Differences

Most human sex-linked behaviors are influenced much more by learning than by biological causes. Most male-female performance gaps can be traced to social differences in power and opportunity.

Gender Identity

Your personal, private sense of being female or male is your gender identity. It begins with how you are labeled at birth.

Gender Role Socialization

Gender roles (culturally favored patterns of behavior expected of each sex) have as big an influence on sexual behavior as any other factor.

Psychological Androgyny

Androgyny refers to the presence of both "masculine" and "feminine" traits in a single person. Androgynous individuals are very adaptable.

Sexual Behavior and Sexual Orientation

Sexuality is a natural part of being human. Sexual orientation is a very basic dimension of sexuality.

Sexual Arousal

Human sexual arousal is complex. Although direct stimulation of the body's erogenous zones (produces arousal), there is a large cognitive element.

Sexual Orientation

Sexual orientation refers to the degree to which you are emotionally and erotically attracted to members of the same sex, opposite sex, or both sexes. A combination of biological and social factors is most likely involved in sexual orientation.

Sexual Scripts

Sexual scripts are unspoken mental plans that guide our sexual behavior. Sexual scripts determine when and where we are likely to express sexual feelings, and with whom.

Sex Drive

The strength of one's motivation to engage in sexual behavior (sex drive) is influenced by attitudes toward sex, sexual experience, how long since sexual activity, and physical factors.

Erogenous Zones

Human erogenous zones include the genitals, mouth, breasts, ears, anus, and to a lesser degree, the entire surface of the body. Beyond just physical contact, human sexual arousal obviously includes a large mental element.

Scripts and Plots

A "script" defines a plot, dialogue, and actions that should take place. Sexual scripts provide a "plot" for the order of events in lovemaking, and they outline "approved" actions, motives, and outcomes.

Masturbation

Masturbation is a basic sexual behavior that is engaged in large percentages of both men and women. Typically, the only negative effects are feelings of fear, guilt, or anxiety that arise from being taught to think of masturbation as "bad" or "wrong."

Heterosexuality

Heterosexual people are romantically attracted to members of the opposite sex.

Homosexuality

Homosexual people are attracted to people whose sex matches their own.

Bisexuality

Bisexual people are attracted to both men and women.

Notes

_____

_____

_____

_____

_____

_____

_____

Sexual Response, Attitudes, and Behavior

An understanding of human sexual response contributes to healthy sexuality.

Human Sexual Response

Sexual responses of both men and women follow four phases (excitement, plateau, orgasm, and resolution).

Excitement Phase
First level of sexual response, indicated by initial signs of sexual arousal.

Plateau Phase
Second level of sexual response, during which physical arousal intensifies.

Orgasm
A climax and release of sexual excitement.

Resolution
The final phase of sexual response, involving a return to lower levels of sexual tension and arousal.

Atypical Sexual Behavior

Public standards and private behavior are often at odds. True sexual deviations are compulsive and destructive.

Exhibitionism
Generally, the goal of an exhibitionist is to shock and alarm the victim.

Paraphilias
Sexual deviations (paraphilias) typically cause feelings of guilt, anxiety, or discomfort for one or both participants.

Child Molestation
The effects of molestation vary. How long it lasts, the type of molestation, and the parents' reactions impact on how severe the emotional harm is.

The Crime of Rape
A recent dramatic increase in date rape (by a forced intercourse in the context of a date has occurred).

Rape Myths
Often a rapist justifies the act by citing one of several widely held beliefs (rape myths).

Forcible Rape
Date rape is coercive but not necessarily violent. Forcible rape is now viewed more as a crime of violence than sex alone.

STDs and Safer Sex

Sexually transmitted diseases (STDs) particularly HIV, are behavioral risk factors. Yet many sexually active people continue to take unnecessary risks with their health by not following safer sex practices.

Chlamydia

Gonorrhea

Hepatitis B

Herpes

HPV (genital warts)

Syphilis

HIV/AIDS

Psychology in Action: Sexual Problems—When Pleasure Fades

Sexual dysfunctions/disorders are far more common than many people realize. Most people who seek sexual counseling have one or more of the following types of problems:

Desire Disorders

Hypoactive Sexual Desire
This condition is characterized by persistent loss of desire plus the person is troubled by it.

Sexual Aversion
This describes a person who is repelled by sex and seeks to avoid it.

Treatment
Treatments include drug therapy, behavioral methods, and counseling.

Arousal Disorders

Male Erectile Disorder
Men with this disorder cannot maintain an erection for lovemaking.

Female Sexual Arousal Disorder
Women who respond with little or no physical arousal to sexual stimulation.

Treatment
Treatment includes behavioral methods and counseling.

Orgasmic Disorders

Female and Male Orgasmic Disorder
This condition describes a person with the persistent inability to reach orgasm during lovemaking.

Premature Ejaculation
Ejaculation is premature if it consistently occurs before the man and his partner want it to occur.

Treatment
Treatment includes behavioral methods, such as the squeeze technique.

Sexual Pain Disorders

Dyspareunia
Dyspareunia involves pain in the genitals before, during. or after sexual intercourse.

Vaginismus
In this condition, muscle spasms of the vagina prevent intercourse.

Treatment
Treatment includes behavioral methods, such as progressive relaxation and counseling.

1. What term refers to all the psychological and social traits associated with being male or female?
   a. Gender
   b. Sex
   c. Sexual category
   d. None of the above.

2. If Donn's biological sex conflicts with his preferred psychological and social gender role, he might be considered a
   a. transvestite.
   b. transsexual.
   c. homosexual.
   d. androgynous.

3. The vagina, ovaries, testes, and penis are all considered _____ _____ sex characteristics.
   a. secondary
   b. fundamental
   c. initial
   d. primary

4. The onset of menstruation in females is referred to as
   a. ovulation.
   b. menopause.
   c. menarche.
   d. a sex difference.

5. Estrogens is to androgens as _____ is to _____.
   a. small; large
   b. female; male
   c. young; old
   d. primary; secondary

6. The text defines classifying someone as male or female as taking into account all of the following except
   a. genetic sex.
   b. genital sex.
   c. gonadal sex.
   d. gender sex.

7. Which of the following combinations of chromosomes would result in male development?
   a. XX
   b. XY
   c. YY
   d. None of the above

8. Being taught by one's culture that hunting is something that men should do is an example of
   a. gender discrimination.
   b. gender stereotyping.
   c. action-oriented learning.
   d. gender role socialization.

9. Oversimplified beliefs about what men and women are actually like are known as
   a. sexual identities.
   b. cognitive gender distortions.
   c. gender role stereotypes.
   d. sex generated roles.

10. If Sally encourages her children to show their emotions, we would say that they are being encouraged in _____ behaviors.
    a. expressive
    b. instrumental
    c. aversive
    d. empathic

11. Tamara describes herself as having both masculine and feminine interests. Because of this, she might be considered as having a high level of
    a. confusion.
    b. androgyny.
    c. reversed role interests.
    d. gender stability.

12. _____ zones are areas of the body that can be directly stimulated for sexual arousal.
    a. Erogenous
    b. Arousal
    c. Stimulation
    d. Sexual orientation

13. Which of the following terms best describes someone who is attracted to both men and women?
    a. Omnisexual
    b. Heterosexual
    c. Homosexual
    d. Bisexual

14. As discussed in the text, rates for teen premarital intercourse have evidenced _____ between 1988 and 2002.
    a. a decrease
    b. an increase
    c. no change
    d. little activity

15. Forced intercourse that occurs in the context of a date or other voluntary encounter is the definition of
    a. acquaintance rape.
    b. date violence.
    c. voluntary rape.
    d. rape stereotyping.

16. Which of the following is not true of STDs?
    a. Many people who carry an STD may not know it.
    b. Sexually active people run a high risk of contracting a STD.
    c. Gonorrhea, herpes, genital warts, and syphilis are examples of STDs.
    d. It is difficult to have an STD infection and not know it.

17. A person experiencing _____ feels fear, anxiety, or disgust about engaging in sex.
    a. a paraphilia
    b. erotic distaste
    c. sexual aversion
    d. erectile dysfunction

18. Sensate focus directs attention to _____ sensations of pleasure and builds _____ skills
    a. erotic; interpersonal
    b. natural; communication
    c. aversive; tolerance
    d. sexual; socialization

19. Which of the following is not one of the ways, identified by Bryan Strong and Christine DeVault (1994), to avoid intimacy?
    a. Never argue.
    b. Never compromise.
    c. Turn off the television.
    d. Take care of your own need first.

20. Barry McCarthy identified all of the following elements necessary for a continuing healthy sexual relationship except
    a. sexual anticipation.
    b. valuing one's sexuality.
    c. believing you don't deserve sexual satisfaction.
    d. valuing intimacy.

MODULE 15.1

Affiliation, Friendship, and Love

Humans are social animals who need contact with family and friends.

Affiliation

The need to affiliate (associate with other people) is based on basic human desires for approval, support, friendship, and information.

Social Comparison Theory

Group membership fills our need for social comparison (comparing our own actions, feelings, opinions, or abilities with those of others). This theory holds that we affiliate to evaluate our actions, feelings, and abilities.

Interpersonal Attraction

Most voluntary social relationships are based on interpersonal attraction. All affect the degree to which we are attracted to others.
- Physical proximity
- Physical attractiveness
- Similarity
- Competence

Factors that Influence Interpersonal Attraction

Self-Disclosure

We find out about similarity by disclosing information about ourselves and finding out information about others. Self-disclosure at a moderate pace builds trust and reciprocity.

Loving and Liking

Romantic love is based on interpersonal attraction with high levels of emotional arousal, sexual desire, and mutual absorption. Liking is affection without passion or deep commitment.

Sex, Evolution, and Mate Selection

Evolutionary psychologists believe that evolution left an imprint on men and women that influences everything from sexual attraction and infidelity to jealousy and divorce.

MODULE 15.2

Groups, Social Influence, and Conformity

To understand social behavior we must know what roles people play, their status, the norms they follow, and the attributions they make.

Group Structure, Cohesion, and Norms

We all belong to many overlapping social groups in which we occupy a position in the structure of the group. Groups have *structure* (a network of roles, communication, and power), *cohesiveness* (a desire to remain in the group), and *norms* (an accepted standard for behavior). Group membership affects our behavior.

Social Roles

Our social roles are patterns of behavior expected of persons in various social positions.

Status

A person's social position within groups determines his or her status, or level of social power and importance. Higher status bestows special privileges and respect.

Norms

Social behavior is affected by group norms. Norms are widely accepted standards for appropriate behavior.

Attributions

We attribute people's behavior to various causes. We infer causes from circumstances.

Social Influence

Social psychologists are very interested in social influence (changes in behavior induced by the actions of others).

Conformity

Group pressure can cause us to conform to the group norm. Nonconformity may be met with group sanctions.

Groupthink

Groupthink is an urge by decision makers to maintain each other's approval, even if critical thinking has to be suspended.

Compliance, Obedience and Self-Assertion

Compliance and obedience to authority are normal parts of social life.

Compliance
Compliance refers to situations in which a person bends to the requests of someone else who has little or no authority.

Low-Ball
The low-ball technique involves getting agreement to a small request and then changing the requirement to a larger situation.

Foot-in-Door
A person who agrees to a small request is more likely to comply with a larger demand later.

Door-in-Face
A person who turns down a large request is more likely to agree to a later, smaller request.

Obedience
Obedience is a special type of conformity to the demands of an authority. Stanley Milgram, social psychologist, conducted a classic study on obedience.

Milgram's Experiment
In Milgram's study, subjects were told to shock a man with a heart condition who was screaming and asking to be released. Sixty-five percent of his subjects "shocked" the man to the extreme, as long as there was a "legitimate authority" to obey.

Milgram's Follow-Up
Milgram found his initial findings disturbing. Consequently, he changed the variables of the study and found lower obedience rates as the distance from the learner and the authority changed.

Implications
Milgram suggested that when directions come from an authority, people rationalize that they are not personally responsible for their actions. Fortunately, he also found the presence of dissenters could free the others to disobey.

Self-Assertion
Self-assertion helps people meet their needs without resorting to aggressive behavior. Self-assertion is a direct, honest expression of feelings and desires. Assertion techniques emphasize firmness, not attack.

Attitudes and Persuasion

Attitudes are intimately woven into our actions and views of the world.

Attitudes
An attitude is a mixture of belief and emotion that predisposes us to respond to other people, objects, or groups in a positive or negative way.

Forming Attitudes
Attitudes may come from direct contact, interaction with others, group membership, child rearing, the mass media, or chance conditioning.

Changing Attitudes
Attitudes are fairly stable, but may change if the reference group (the group used for social comparison) changes.

Attitudes and Behavior
Some attitudes may not be acted upon because of the consequences of the behavior (public reaction), or old habits, or lack of conviction.

Persuasion
Persuasion is any deliberate attempt to change attitudes or beliefs through information and arguments. Persuasion can be enhanced by a variety of known techniques.

Brainwashing
Brainwashing (forced attitude change) requires a captive audience that can be made to feel totally helpless and dependent on the captor.

Cults
Cults employ high-pressure techniques similar to brainwashing to gain control of cult members.

Cognitive Dissonance Theory
This theory states that contradicting or clashing thoughts cause discomfort. Efforts to resolve the inconsistency may result in attitude change.

Prejudice and Intergroup Conflict

Prejudice, marked by suspicion, fear, or hatred, breaks people apart. Unfortunately, it is an all-too-common part of daily life.

Prejudice

Prejudice is a *negative emotional attitude* held toward members of a specific social group. Prejudices may be reflected in the policies of organizations and may be referred to as *racism*, *sexism*, *ageism*, or *heterosexism*, depending on the group affected.

Origins of Prejudice

Prejudice may lead to discrimination (the behavioral element of the attitude).

Scapegoating

Here, a person or a group is blamed for the actions of others or for conditions not of their making, also known as displaced aggression.

Personal Prejudice

This occurs when members of another ethnic group are perceived as a threat to one's own interests.

Group Prejudice

This occurs when a person conforms to group norms.

Prejudiced Personality

Prejudice can be a general personality characteristic (authoritarian, ethnocentric, and concerned with power).

Intergroup Conflict

Shared beliefs concerning *superiority*, *injustice*, *vulnerability*, and *distrust* are common triggers for hostility between groups.

Reducing Prejudice

Any of these methods can be used to reduce prejudice and increase tolerance.

Combating Prejudice

Research has shown that prejudice can be reduced by the following methods:

Equal-Status Contact

When social groups interact on an equal footing, without obvious differences in power or status.

Superordinate Goals

The establishment of goals that override other lesser goals, forcing cooperation among members of both groups, reduces prejudice.

Mutual Interdependence

Having to depend on one another to meet each person's goals can lessen prejudice.

Jigsaw Classrooms

When each student is given a "piece" of the information needed to complete a project or prepare for a test, students from different social groups display less prejudice.

Aggression and Prosocial Behavior

Reducing violence and increasing prosocial behavior are pressing issues.

Aggression

Aggression refers to any action carried out with the intention of harming another person.

Instincts

The idea that humans are naturally aggressive is rejected by many psychologists.

Biology

Aggression may have some biological roots in brain areas.

Frustration

Frustration may lead to aggression; however, frustration can also lead to other behaviors.

Aversive Stimuli

Aversive stimuli, which are unpleasant, can heighten hostility and aggression.

Social Learning

Aggression may be learned in a social situation or demonstrated by aggressive models (including television).

Prosocial Behavior

Prosocial behaviors include actions that are constructive, altruistic, or helpful to others.

Bystander Intervention

For bystander intervention to occur a bystander must: notice the need, interpret an emergency, decide to take responsibility, and select a course of action.

Who Helps?

When we see a person in trouble, it tends to cause heightened arousal. Potential helpers may feel empathetic arousal, and there is a strong empathy-helping relationship.

Psychology in Action: Multiculturalism—Living with Diversity

How can tolerance be encouraged?

Break the Prejudice Habit

Value openness to the other, the ability to genuinely appreciate those who differ from us culturally.

Beware of Stereotyping

Make the effort to tear down stereotypes, emphasize fairness and equality, and get to know people from various ethnic and cultural groups.

Seek Individuating Information

Seek information that helps us see a person as an individual, rather than as a member of a group.

Don't Fall Prey to Just-World Beliefs

Believing that the world is sufficiently just so that people generally get what they deserve can directly increase prejudiced thinking.

Be Aware of Self-Fulfilling Prophecies

Beware of having expectations that prompt people to act in ways that make the expectations come true.

Remember, Different Does Not Mean Inferior

It is not necessary to degrade other groups in order to feel positive about one's own group identity.

Understand That Race Is a Social Construction

Race is an illusion based on superficial physical differences and learned ethnic identities.

Look for Commonalities

Overcome the need to demean, defeat, and vanquish others. Try to cooperate with others so as to share their joys and suffer their sorrows.

Set an Example for Others

Act in a tolerant fashion so you can serve as a model of tolerance for others.

1. _____ is the scientific study of how individuals behave, think, and feel in social situations
   a. Social psychology
   b. Sociology
   c. Psychology
   d. Intrapersonal psychology

2. Although Mia was not happy, initially, with her midterm grade, when she found out that all her friends' grades were lower she began to feel better about her grade. A social psychologist would accurately refer to this change in belief as a result of social
   a. association.
   b. assessment.
   c. comparison.
   d. relativity.

3. Physical proximity promotes attraction due to increases in
   a. similarity of interests.
   b. frequency of contact.
   c. initial contact.
   d. social interaction.

4. The process of disclosing private thoughts and feelings and revealing yourself to others is referred to as
   a. interpersonal release.
   b. mutual absorption.
   c. romantic love.
   d. self-disclosure.

5. "Husband" and "psychologist" would be examples of _____ roles.
   a. ascribed
   b. achieved
   c. conflicted
   d. primary

6. What is the term for the degree of attraction among group members or the strength of their desire to remain in the group?
   a. Group cohesiveness
   b. Group structure
   c. Intergroup appeal
   d. None of the above.

7. Devon considers himself a big Detroit Lions fan and identifies with other Lions fans. He also despises the Chicago Bears and cannot understand why anyone would want to be a fan of that team. For Devon, other Detroit Lions fans would be considered a(n) _____, whereas Chicago Bears fans would be a(n) _____.
   a. out-group, in-group
   b. social support, social threat
   c. benefit, detriment
   d. in-group, out-group

8. Allison always stands during the playing of the national anthem. This standard for appropriate behavior would be considered by social psychologists a
   a. standard.
   b. norm.
   c. social rule.
   d. value set.

9. Dennis gets "cut off" on the highway while driving to class. His first belief is that the person driving the other car was rude and self-absorbed. He does not consider the situational influences that may have affected the driver's actions. Dennis has committed
   a. self-serving biasing.
   b. the fundamental attribution error.
   c. actor-observer bias.
   d. cognitive reversal.

10. "Because we have always been in agreement in the past, I hope we will be able to agree this time as well" is a statement one might hear if _____ is occurring.
   a. obedience
   b. group bias
   c. attribution
   d. groupthink

11. John was asked by the salesman to "simply take the car for a drive around the block." This request would be considered an example of the _____ effect.
   a. foot-in-the-door
   b. door-in-the-face
   c. low-ball
   d. door-to-door

12. Stanley Milgram's experiments, in which a subject gave varying degrees of shocks to a "learner," demonstrated the effects of the situation on the subject's
   a. obedience.
   b. understanding.
   c. stress levels.
   d. acceptance.

13. The three basic rights of assertiveness training include all of the following except
   a. the right to request.
   b. the right to refuse.
   c. the right to restitution.
   d. the right to right a wrong.

14. _____, as defined by the text, involves hurting another person or achieving one's goals at the expense of another.
   a. Violence
   b. Hostility
   c. Assertion
   d. Aggression

15. _____ is any deliberate attempt to change attitudes or beliefs through information and arguments.
   a. Persuasion
   b. Conformity
   c. Compliance
   d. Obedience

16. Glenna bought a new car even though she had already decided that she would only buy a used car. Because of this contradiction in her thoughts and behaviors, she is now experiencing increased anxiety. This anxiety may be a result of what social psychologists refer to as
   a. a personal neurosis.
   b. behavioral conflict.
   c. cognitive dissonance.
   d. groupthink.

17. Prejudice is to discrimination as _____ is to _____.
   a. secondary; primary
   b. attitude; behavior
   c. primary; secondary
   d. behavior; attitude

18. _____ simplify(ies) people by putting them into categories.
   a. Social labeling
   b. Cultural blindness
   c. Biases
   d. Stereotypes

19. Darley and Latané believe that in order for people to help someone else, they must
   a. notice that something is happening.
   b. define the event as an emergency.
   c. take responsibility.
   d. do all of the above.

20. Because Todd believed that he could not pass the final exam, he did very little to prepare for it. His eventual failure on the exam could be considered an example of a
   a. self-fulfilling prophecy.
   b. self-serving bias.
   c. just-world effect.
   d. social competition.

Chapter 16

Applied Psychology

Industrial/Organizational Psychology

Industrial/organizational (I/O) psychologists study the behavior of people at work.

Theories of Leadership
Two basic leadership theories are often found in the workplace.

Organizational Culture
Culture refers to a blend of customs, beliefs, values, attitudes, and rituals that give each organization its unique "flavor."

Personnel Psychology
Personnel psychologists are concerned with testing, selection, placement, and promotion of employees.

Theory X Leaders
Use scientific management.

Emphasis on work efficiency.

Task orientation

Assume workers must be goaded or guided into being productive.

Low Job Satisfaction
Low job satisfaction is linked with high absenteeism, low morale, and high employee turnover, which leads to higher training costs and inefficiency.

Theory Y Leaders
Use shared leadership and management by objectives.

Emphasis on human relations at work.

People orientation

Assume workers enjoy autonomy, responsibility, industry, creativity, and challenging work.

High Job Satisfaction
High job satisfaction is linked with better cooperation, better performance, greater willingness to help others, more creative problem solving, and less absenteeism.

Organizational Citizenship
Workers who are helpful, conscientious, courteous, and avoid pettiness and gossip, are highly valued by their leaders.

Job Analysis
Job analysis (a detailed description of the skills, knowledge, and activities required by a job) is the first step in personnel selection.

Selection Procedures
Once desirable skills and traits are known, the next step is to find people who have these abilities. Biodata, interviews, and psychological tests may be used.

Four Coping Styles for Dissatisfied Workers
Four basic coping styles these workers are common for workers with extreme job dissatisfaction.
- The vigilant style: The most effective style, these workers evaluate information objectively and make decisions by reviewing alternatives.
- The complacent style: Workers with this style let chance direct their careers with no planning.
- The defensive-avoidant style: Defensive-avoidant workers procrastinate due to indecision, rationalize, and make excuses for inaction and indecision.
- The hypervigilant style: Hypervigilant workers panic when forced to make career decisions.

Environmental Psychology

Environmental psychology is a specialty concerned with the relationship between environments and human behavior. Environmental psychologists are interested in both physical environments and social environments.

Social Environments and Behavioral Settings

Social environments are defined by groups of people, such as a dance, business meeting, or party. Behavioral settings are smaller areas within an environment whose use is well defined.

Personal Space

Personal space is our individual envelope which we regard as private. The systematic study of rules for use of personal space is called *proxemics*.

Spatial Norms

In North America, social distances are:
- Intimate (0-18 inches)
- Personal (18 inches to 4 feet)
- Social (4-12 feet)
- Public (12 feet plus)

Territoriality

Personal space extends to our "territory, the area we consider ours." Note how students "claim" a seat in classrooms.

Physical Environments

Physical environments are natural or constructed.

Stressful Environments

Overcrowding, traffic congestion, high-noise areas, toxic environments, and declining resources all contribute to stress-laden environments.

Crowding

Crowding refers to the subjective feelings of being over-stimulated by social inputs or loss of privacy.

Noise

Noise pollution, annoying and intrusive noise, is a major source of environmental stress.

Toxic Environments

Human activities drastically change the natural environment. Examples include deforestation, burning fossil fuels, and chemical usage.

Environmental Problem Solving

Environmental psychologists are working on ways to educate and motivate people to act in ways that create healthier environments.
- Reduce, reuse, recycle
- Educate
- Provide money rewards
- Remove barriers
- Use persuasion
- Seek public commitment
- Encourage goal setting
- Give feedback
- Revise attitudes

The Psychology of Law and Sports

Psychology can be seen in action at courthouses and sporting events.

Psychology and Law

The psychology of law is the study of the behavioral dimensions of the legal system.

Jury Behavior

Psychologists use mock juries to help understand what determines how real juries vote.

Jury Problems

Research shows jurors:
- are not able to put aside biases and values.
- are not good at separating evidence from other information.
- are influenced by inadmissible evidence.
- are not able to suspend judgment until all evidence is presented.

Jury Selection

Many attorneys use psychologists to assist in scientific jury selection using social science principles.

Death-Qualified Juries

Members of a death-qualified jury must favor the death penalty (or at least be indifferent to it). Such juries have a higher than average conviction rate.

Sports Psychology

Sports psychology is the study of the behavioral dimensions of sports performance.

Task Analysis

By doing a task analysis, sports skills can be broken into subparts in order to identify key elements and teach them to the competitor. Focus is on motor skill refinement.

Positive Psychology

During peak performance, physical, mental, and emotional states are in harmony and are optimal. Psychologists are seeking to identify conditions that facilitate peak performance.

Notes

_____

_____

_____

_____

_____

_____

_____

Psychology in Action: Human Factors Psychology—Who's the Boss Here?

Human factors psychology helps create machines that are more user friendly. The goal of human factors psychology, also known as *ergonomics*, is to design machines and work environments so they are compatible with our sensory and motor capacities.

Usability Testing

Usability testing involves the measurement of ease with which people can learn to use a machine.

Use of Natural Design

Natural design makes use of perceptual signals that people understand naturally.

Human-Computer Interaction

HCI involves using human factors methods to design computers and software.

Using Tools Effectively

When using tools, one should understand the task first, then attempt to understand the tool. Beware of satisficing.

Notes

_____

_____

_____

_____

_____

_____

_____

1. _____ refers to the use of psychological principles and research methods to solve practical problems.
   a. Practical psychology
   b. Social psychology
   c. Organizational psychology
   d. Applied psychology

2. Chad's job is to assist companies in identifying ways in which their workers could become more efficient. Chad would most accurately be identified as a(n) _____ psychologist.
   a. professional
   b. organizational
   c. social
   d. clinical

3. The idea that "happy workers are productive workers" demonstrates the importance of _____.
   a. psychological efficiency
   b. work efficiency
   c. morale efficiency
   d. work humor efficiency

4. Joy is considered a people person and typically assumes that her employees prefer independence and are willing to accept personal responsibility in their jobs. Joy would most likely be considered a _____ leader.
   a. Theory Y
   b. Theory X
   c. personable
   d. scientific

5. A group of employees who work together toward a shared goal are referred to as a(n)
   a. objective-managed team.
   b. shared-leadership team.
   c. self-managed team.
   d. participative-managed team.

6. _____ is the degree to which a person is pleased with his or her work.
   a. Work contentment
   b. Job enrichment
   c. Employment appeal
   d. Job satisfaction

7. In his job at the factory, Steve works 10 hours per day but only 4 days per week. This practice is known as
   a. practice management.
   b. flex time.
   c. a compressed work week.
   d. work condensation.

8. Which of the following is not one of the four coping styles described by Wheeler and Janis?
   a. Hypervigilant
   b. Vigilante
   c. Defensive-avoidant
   d. Complacent

9. _____ psychology is concerned with testing, selection, placement, and promotion of employees.
   a. Personnel
   b. Personality
   c. Person-centered
   d. Personal

10. The use of an employee's past behavior to predict future behavior is the idea behind _____.
    a. biopsychosocial data collection
    b. profiling
    c. attrition theory
    d. biodata

11. Which of the following is not one of the recommendations made by the U.S. Department of Labor for surviving a job interview?
    a. Consider possible questions and outline your specific answers.
    b. Do not chew gum.
    c. Be on time.
    d. Avoid the use of slang terms.

12. The *Kuder Occupational Interest Survey* and the *Strong-Campbell Interest Inventory* are examples of what kind of test?
    a. Employment aptitude tests
    b. Vocational interest tests
    c. Computerized tests
    d. Occupational interest inventories

13. *Proxemics* is the systematic study of rules for the use of
    a. verbal communication.
    b. personality tests.
    c. public speaking.
    d. personal space.

14. What did Stanley Milgram identify as a result of overcrowding and high-density populations?
    a. Hostile motivation
    b. Cognitive overload
    c. Attentional overload
    d. Intentional excess

15. The volume of greenhouse gases each individual's consumption adds to the atmosphere is referred to as the
    a. carbon footprint.
    b. carbon neutral lifestyle.
    c. carbon debit.
    d. carbon meter.

16. The text identifies all of the following responses for lightening the environmental impact of our "throw-away" society, except
    a. recycling materials.
    b. reproducing attitudes.
    c. reducing consumption.
    d. reusing products.

17. In order to understand the possible behaviors one might observe within a jury setting, psychologist employ the use of _____.
    a. mock juries
    b. scientific juries
    c. replicated juries
    d. simulated juries

18. What attitude must a death-qualified juror typically have toward the death penalty?
    a. Against
    b. In favor of
    c. Unaware of
    d. All of the above are possible.

19. _____ is the study of the behavioral dimensions of sports performance.
    a. Game theory
    b. Aerobic empiricism
    c. Exercise science
    d. Sports psychology

20. Driving a car, putting a golf ball, playing drums, and even typing your research paper are all examples of
    a. motor skills.
    b. motor abilities.
    c. motor programs.
    d. motor competition.

Descriptive Statistics

Descriptive statistics summarize numbers so they become more meaningful and easier to communicate to others.

Graphical Statistics

Summarizing data pictorially (graphically) helps us to envision the results.

Z-Score

A z-score is a number that tells how many standard deviations above or below the mean a score is.

Normal Curve

A normal distribution curve is often found when recording chance events shows that some outcomes have a high probability and occur very often, whereas others occur less often.

Measures of Central Tendency

Central tendency measures include the following:
- *Mean*–the average of all scores.
- *Median*–the middle score.
- *Mode*–the score that occurs most often.

Measures of Variability

Variability measures include the following:
- *Range*–the difference between the highest and lowest scores.
- *Standard deviation*–how much scores deviate from the mean of a group of scores.

Inferential Statistics

Inferential statistics are techniques that allow us to make inferences, to generalize from samples and draw conclusions.

Samples and Population

Samples (smaller cross sections of a population) allow us to make inferences about the whole population.

Representative and Random

Samples are most valid when they truly reflect the membership and characteristics of the larger population.

Significant Differences

Tests of *statistical significance* provide an estimate of how often experimental results could have occurred by chance alone.

Correlation

Correlations tell us about the relationship between two variables. Knowledge about one factor allows us to make *predictions* concerning the other factor.

Correlation vs. Causation

It is important to understand that correlation does not demonstrate causation.

Behavioral Statistics

Practice Exam

1. Summary is to conclusion as _____ is to
   _____.
   a. validity; reliability
   b. descriptive; inferential
   c. reliability; validity
   d. inferential; descriptive

2. All of the following are examples of graphical statistics except
   a. frequency distribution.
   b. frequency polygon.
   c. inferential polygram.
   d. histogram.

3. In his attempt to identify the central tendency of test scores
   within his classroom, what could Larry calculate?
   a. Mode
   b. Median
   c. Mean
   d. All of the above.

4. A standard deviation is considered a measure of _____.
   a. variability
   b. reliability
   c. validity
   d. central tendency

5. The distribution of many naturally occurring characteristics is
   often represented by
   a. an inverted U.
   b. a z-line.
   c. a normal curve.
   d. None of the above.

6. _____ statistics allow us to generalize behaviors
   of a relatively small group of individuals to that of a larger group.
   a. Simplified
   b. Deductive
   c. Inferential
   d. Descriptive

7. If for every additional bowl of Wheatios cereal eaten each day,
   your cholesterol dropped 5 points, we would conclude
   a. that a perfect positive correlational relationship exists.
   b. that it is by mere chance and no relationship exists.
   c. that a causal relationship exists.
   d. that a perfect negative correlational relationship exists.

8. Tests of _____ provide an estimate of how often
   experimental results could have occurred by chance alone.
   a. representative transference.
   b. correlational coefficients
   c. random assignment
   d. statistical significance

9. If Tashana has a score on her exam of 130, with the average
   score for the class being 120 and a standard deviation of 10, her
   z-score would be _____.
   a. +1.0
   b. +0.1
   c. −1.0
   d. −0.1

10. In order for a representative sample to be considered _____,
    each member of the population must have an equal chance of
    being involved in the sample.
    a. causal
    b. co-relating
    c. significant
    d. random

ANSWERS TO PRACTICE EXAMS

Chapter 1: Introducing Psychology and Research Methods
1. a	5. a	9. c	13. a	17. c
2. c	6. d	10. b	14. c	18. a
3. b	7. b	11. a	15. b	19. c
4. c	8. a	12. c	16. a	20. b

Chapter 2: Brain and Behavior
1. a	5. b	9. c	13. a	17. d
2. c	6. b	10. d	14. a	18. b
3. b	7. c	11. b	15. c	19. c
4. d	8. a	12. b	16. a	20. c

Chapter 3: Human Development
1. b	5. c	9. c	13. d	17. a
2. a	6. d	10. d	14. b	18. b
3. c	7. b	11. a	15. c	19. c
4. a	8. d	12. c	16. b	20. d

Chapter 4: Sensation and Perception
1. b	5. c	9. a	13. b	17. d
2. b	6. c	10. b	14. c	18. a
3. d	7. a	11. d	15. d	19. b
4. b	8. d	12. c	16. a	20. a

Chapter 5: States of Consciousness
1. d	5. d	9. b	13. b	17. a
2. d	6. b	10. a	14. a	18. b
3. a	7. a	11. a	15. d	19. b
4. a	8. d	12. c	16. b	20. b

Chapter 6: Conditioning and Learning
1. a	5. b	9. a	13. b	17. b
2. d	6. a	10. b	14. d	18. c
3. d	7. d	11. a	15. b	19. d
4. b	8. c	12. a	16. d	20. c

Chapter 7: Memory
1. c	5. a	9. a	13. b	17. c
2. b	6. a	10. d	14. d	18. b
3. d	7. c	11. a	15. b	19. c
4. d	8. d	12. d	16. b	20. c

Chapter 8: Intelligence, Cognition, Language, and Creativity
1. c	5. d	9. b	13. d	17. a
2. c	6. d	10. a	14. c	18. c
3. c	7. a	11. d	15. b	19. b
4. a	8. c	12. c	16. b	20. a

Chapter 9: Motivation and Emotion
1. c	5. a	9. b	13. c	17. c
2. d	6. c	10. a	14. d	18. d
3. b	7. b	11. d	15. a	19. a
4. b	8. d	12. d	16. c	20. b

Chapter 10: Personality
1. b	5. a	9. b	13. a	17. b
2. a	6. c	10. d	14. b	18. a
3. d	7. a	11. c	15. c	19. c
4. c	8. d	12. c	16. c	20. a

Chapter 11: Health, Stress, and Coping
1. b	5. a	9. d	13. a	17. b
2. a	6. b	10. d	14. d	18. c
3. d	7. a	11. d	15. c	19. c
4. d	8. d	12. c	16. a	20. d

Chapter 12: Psychological Disorders
1. b	5. a	9. d	13. b	17. b
2. c	6. a	10. b	14. a	18. c
3. a	7. c	11. c	15. d	19. a
4. c	8. a	12. a	16. c	20. a

Chapter 13: Therapies
1. c	5. c	9. c	13. a	17. b
2. a	6. c	10. b	14. d	18. c
3. c	7. a	11. d	15. c	19. b
4. a	8. b	12. c	16. c	20. d

Chapter 14: Gender and Sexuality
1. a	5. b	9. c	13. d	17. c
2. b	6. d	10. a	14. a	18. b
3. d	7. b	11. b	15. a	19. c
4. c	8. d	12. a	16. d	20. c

Chapter 15: Social Behavior
1. a	5. b	9. b	13. c	17. b
2. c	6. a	10. d	14. a	18. d
3. b	7. d	11. a	15. a	19. d
4. d	8. b	12. a	16. c	20. a

Chapter 16: Applied Psychology
1. d	5. c	9. a	13. d	17. a
2. b	6. d	10. d	14. c	18. b
3. a	7. c	11. a	15. a	19. d
4. a	8. b	12. b	16. b	20. a

Appendix: Behavioral Statistics
1. b	5. c	9. a
2. c	6. c	10. d
3. d	7. d	
4. a	8. d